TAKE YOUR CA ABROAD

NIGEL FRYATT

**Photography by
Gordon Cole**

IAN ALLAN Publishing

First published 1993

ISBN 0 7110 2053 1

© Nigel Fryatt 1993

Nigel Fryatt has asserted his
right to be identified as the
author of this work.

Published by Ian Allan Ltd,
Shepperton, Surrey; and
printed by Ian Allan Printing
Ltd at their works at
Coombelands in Runnymede,
England.

The author and publishers
have made every effort to
ensure that all information
given in this publication is
accurate at the time of writing
but can accept no
consequential responsibility
for errors or omissions. Legal
requirements, traffic
regulations, and other matters
may be subject to change and
no statement in this book
should be understood as
giving definitive information in
any such respect.

Contents

Acknowledgements

Nigel Fryatt would like
to thank the information
services of both the AA
and RAC who assisted
substantially in the
research for this book.

The majority of the
photographs included in
this book were taken by
Gordon Cole, additional
picture credits are
noted in the captions.
Gordon Cole and the
publishers would like to
thank Vauxhall Motors
Ltd who kindly supplied
vehicles, and P&O
European Ferries and
Sealink Stena Line for
assistance with ferries.

Introduction

If you enjoy your motoring, then there must be times when you find the UK very frustrating. Yes, you can find some lovely touring areas in this country, but it is all too often far too congested.

Now Europe is a big place. Unfortunately, the British 'island mentality' has always left us with something of an 'us and them' philosophy. I have never fully understood this, and I have never understood why more people don't take their cars abroad for long touring holidays, for weekends, even just for day trips. Driving in Europe should hold no fears; driving in Europe is rewarding, enjoyable and great fun for all the family.

What we have tried to do with this publication is to offer you a 'passport' to 24 different destinations. They range from our neighbours, France, to far away Turkey and from the British outpost of Gibraltar, to the mysterious lands of eastern Europe. I have been lucky enough personally to visit all but five of the countries mentioned and have clocked up many thousands of miles driving throughout the Continent of Europe. It's a delight to take your car and travel across borders and experience different customs. You don't need to be anything other than a confident driver and follow our advice before you leave, to be reasonably sure of a trouble free trip. Of course, you may have problems, but hopefully these will be minor and we have offered advice of what to do in the event of a breakdown or accident.

My final word or warning, however, is aimed at anyone who decides to travel to Europe by car for the very first time. You'll want to go back. Again and again.

Nigel Fryatt

Planning the Trip

BEFORE YOU GO...

All the best journeys start at home. With some careful planning and simple vehicle checks you can avoid many of the problems that might otherwise ruin your European adventure.

Taking your car, complete with family or friends, into Europe need not be a step into the great unknown. It does not need to be planned with the precision of a military operation, but some simple preparations are necessary to ensure a trouble-free trip.

Firstly, make sure that all persons travelling have up to date, valid **passports**. There is so much more freedom throughout Europe that you may be able to drive through border posts without being stopped at all, and even when you are stopped, the cursory glance at UK passports may even make you wonder why you bothered. But make sure you do. If you do not hold a UK passport, check visa requirements with the appropriate embassies of the countries you intend to visit, before you leave.

The next important piece of documentation after the passport is obviously your **driving licence**. A full UK licence (not Provisional) is valid in most European countries but there are a few exceptions so check by reading the specific country details that follow. In some countries, the minimum age for driving is 18. It is also sensible to invest in an **International Driving Permit** as this is easily obtainable and recognised throughout Europe. The difference from your National licence is that the IDP carries your photograph and full translations of your details. You can obtain an IDP from offices of the major motoring associations. You will need two passport sized photographs and to pay a small fee. The IDP is valid for a year and cannot be renewed — you will need to get a brand new one next year. One most important point is to keep your licence and IDP with you at all times. If you are stopped you will be expected to produce your licence immediately, telling the local police that it is back in your hotel will not do.

You must also carry a **Vehicle Registration Document** for your vehicle, to prove that you have the right to be driving it. If it is your privately owned vehicle this is no problem, however, if it is a hire car you must tell the company where you intend to take the vehicle. Similarly, if the vehicle is your company car, ensure you have the correct documentation linking you with the vehicle to show you are entitled to drive it. If you have just changed the vehicle and not got the official Vehicle Registration Document, you can apply at your local Vehicle Registration Office for a Certificate of Registration (V379). This is acknowledged internationally in lieu of the VRD.

Always contact your broker or motor insurer before you leave the country. Throughout Europe, Third Party Risk insurance is compulsory. Most UK motor insurance policies cover this minimum legal requirement but it is always worth checking to notify your insurer of your plans. This is particularly important if, for instance, you will have someone in the car who may do some of the driving but does not usually drive the car in the UK. It can be a mere formality to check that your best friend is insured to drive your car. Failing to do so, however, may mean he or she stops being a best friend before the trip is over.

Going Abroad?

Taking Your Car?

Then General Accident's *Motor Breakdown & Travel Policy* is just the ticket. It's been specially designed for driving holidays to protect your car, your family and your belongings whilst abroad.

And make sure you take a green card with you, to extend your comprehensive motor insurance to most EC countries. Don't assume your existing insurance will apply.

For more details, visit your local General Accident office or your insurance adviser.

And once you're home again, remember - General Accident has a full range of policies designed to meet most of your insurance requirements.

GA

General Accident

BEAM BENDERS

UNIVERSAL HEADLAMP CONVERTERS FOR CONTINENTAL DRIVING

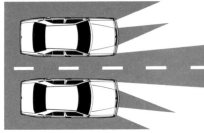

CONVERTS YOUR DIPPED BEAM FROM THE LEFT – FOR DRIVING IN GREAT BRITAIN . . . **GB**

TO THE RIGHT – FOR DRIVING ON THE CONTINENT. **EEC**

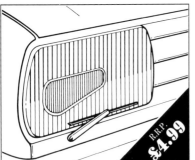

R.R.P. $4.99

Beam Benders are universal headlamp converters for continental driving. One size fits most vehicles. Unlike other products Beam Benders do not block out light, they simply re-direct it at the correct angle. They are optically designed contact lenses which cover the area on the headlamps from which the dipped beam emerges. Beam Benders are self-adhesive and simply stick onto the glass without the need for cutting, trimming or painting. No technical knowledge is required and they can be **FITTED IN SECONDS.** Being only 1mm thick, they will not impede the use of headlamp wash/wipe systems.

STOPLOCK®

UNIVERSAL STEERING IMMOBILIZER

100% SUCCESS RATE IN POLICE TEST

R.R.P. $29.95

In an independent long term test conducted jointly by West Midlands Police and Birmingham City Council, STOPLOCK proved 100% effective in preventing car theft.*

Proof indeed that STOPLOCK really works. STOPLOCK is a **highly visible, easy to use,** steering immobilizer. It consists of a high grade steel bar, coated with a soft outer covering, which locks onto and through the steering wheel. This effectively immobilizes any vehicle so that it cannot be driven away by joy riders and thieves. STOPLOCK is Britain's top selling immobilizer.

*(Official test results available from West Midlands Police)

METRO PRODUCTS

Available from good accessory shops, or contact

Metro Products,
118 Station Rd. East,
Oxted Surrey RH8 0QA
(0883) 717644

We strongly recommend that you take an **International Motor Insurance Certificate** — more commonly known as a **Green Card** — even if it is not a legal requirement everywhere. It will often prove much more useful than a UK insurance certificate. It is recognised throughout Europe and that will make a lot of sense if you are stopped by a local policeman in the back of beyond, late at night. The Green Card carries both the vehicle's details and the named drivers. It certainly makes sense, especially in eastern Europe. If Spain is on your list of countries to be visited, make sure you have a **Bail Bond** since a traffic accident, even if minor, can have quite serious consequences without one (see page 89 for further details). You can obtain a Green Card from your insurer/broker.

We go into more detail about accident and breakdown insurance later in this section. It is definitely worth considering taking some form of additional insurance cover especially if your journey through Europe is going to be a long one and you intend travelling to the far corners of the Continent. This is particularly significant with medical insurance. If nothing else, it will give you peace of mind throughout the trip.

We also list the various drink-driving regulations in the country sections. These do vary and are often stricter than in the UK. The best advice is never to drink and drive under any circumstances.

PREPARING THE CAR

There are those who consider filling up the car with fuel and throwing a passport into the glove box is all the preparation necessary before travelling abroad. Well-maintained modern cars are generally reliable but a little care before you go could save a lot of problems later. The areas to concentrate on are electrical/ignition systems, fuel and cooling systems. Starting with the electrical systems, when was the last time you checked that all the lights worked properly? That has to be the first step, and the heart of the electrical system is the battery. The main problems here relate to the connections. Corrosion round the terminals will often lead to a break in the circuit, so make sure these are clean and smear some petroleum jelly on the terminals to keep them that way. Ensure that the battery is located securely and that the earth connection to the car is clear of corrosion. If the battery is one that can be refilled, check the level and top up with distilled water where necessary.

Do you know where your car's fuse box is located? Check this out and see if it carries any spare fuses. If the answer is no, buy a selection of spares. This particular precaution costs so little but can save you so much in the event of a blown fuse. And while you are buying the **fuses**, include a set of **replacement bulbs** for your vehicle. This is compulsory in some European countries and advisable in all of them. You will also need **headlamp beam deflector** lens covers or 'stick-on' headlamp beam adjusters. These alter the direction of the light pattern which is necessary since you will be driving on the right-hand side of the road in a car set up to dip its lights to the left. It will stop you being flashed at by a lot of angry European motorists, or worse, being fined by the local police.

When it comes to the fuel system there is little you can do as a precaution if you have a modern fuel injected car. A good service before you leave will have to do, since modern fuel injection systems baffle all but the most enthusiastic DIY mechanics. Some simple checks can be made, however, for both fuel injected and carburettor cars. Look carefully at all rubber fuel lines searching for cracking or signs of leakage. If your vehicle has a fuel filter, check its condition and clean thoroughly or replace if necessary. If, during investigation, you notice evidence of fuel leaking from or around the carburettor it would be worth having this checked at a professional workshop. This will ensure your car is running with the correct fuel mixture, essential if you are to depart on a long journey. A good tip is to carry a spare safety fuel can since the frequency of fuel stations in Europe does vary from country to country. You should also check our country list, however, since it is illegal to carry fuel in a can in a few European countries.

Besides the fuel can, make sure you have a simple tool kit for emergencies and check the condition of the spare wheel, wheelbrace and jack and jacking points

Your car's cooling system is probably going to be under far more strain than normal so it is worth a good check over before you leave. Climatic changes will obviously effect your car's system, and you may well be travelling far greater distances in one go than the car is used to. Check all coolant hoses for signs of ageing. This is usually highlighted with bulges or blisters in the hose. It's no good 'thinking' it will be OK, replace it now. That will mean you have to drain the radiator which is no bad thing since that will allow you to put in the recommended anti-freeze solution. In your kit of useful tools and spares, slip in some spare hose and some all-important screw tight hose clips.

NECESSARY ACCESSORIES

All cars must have an approved **GB plate** fixed to the rear. Failure to display one can lead to a fine, which is a rather silly way to spend your holiday money.

You will also need a **warning triangle**. It is compulsory in Austria, Belgium, Bulgaria, Czechoslovakia, Denmark, France, Germany, Greece, Hungary, Italy, Luxembourg, Netherlands, Poland, Portugal and Romania and it is highly advisable for Finland, Norway, Sweden and Switzerland. You have to place the triangle to warn approaching traffic should you break down or have an accident. Make sure you buy a good quality warning triangle and one that also has a list of the specific distances and positions that apply in different countries. The bonus is also that it makes a lot of sense to carry one when driving back in the UK.

The law on **fire extinguishers** only really relates to Bulgaria, Greece and Turkey where it is compulsory to carry one. However, it is strongly to be recommended that one is carried at all times whatever the country.

A **First Aid Kit** is compulsory for Austria, Bulgaria, Czechoslovakia, Greece and Romania. But, once again, it is advisable to carry one at all times in all countries.

Bearing in mind that you will be driving on the right, if your

We cannot promise that it will always be empty as this route through Provence, France, but Europe is a big place and generally motorway congestion is not up to M25 proportions. AA Photo Library.

vehicle does not have an external rear view **mirror on the left** side of the vehicle, it is advisable to have one fitted. This need only be of the clip-on variety, but it will certainly help your driving immensely.

If you feel it all a little complicated to purchase all this equipment, you can hire an emergency travel kit from both the AA and RAC. The hire fee is not excessive and is obviously an excellent way of making sure you have everything. The major motoring organisations also offer a roof rack, with or without storage box, and bike rack hire service that does prove very popular.

MAP IT OUT

It is essential that you take comprehensive maps with you. It is obviously possible to buy these in the country or countries that you visit, but a great selection of maps is available in the UK. It is much better to plan routes and estimate how long any journey will take before you go. There are a large number of European map books available especially from the two top motoring organisations, the AA and RAC. Michelin also publish their excellent maps in the UK. Although perhaps a trifle complicated when first looked at, Michelin maps are crammed with all the information that you could possibly want to plan your route.

If you want someone else to plan the route for you, then both the AA and RAC offer this service. The AA European Routes Service is available for members and non-members. You need only state the starting point and destination to get a full computer print-out of the AA's advised route. It is available by post or can be ordered from any AA shop.

The RAC offers a similar service with its European Route and Travel Pack. As with the AA service, you can choose whether you want the most direct motorway route between two points, a non-motorway route or the most picturesque route. This will allow you to consider avoiding all toll roads to save money — but this will naturally take longer. If you are a seasoned traveller, you can obtain town maps from the RAC without the extra details of how to get there. Again these are available from RAC offices or direct by post.

FERRY CROSSINGS

Any journey from the UK to Europe starts at the ferry terminal. And that in itself can be quite a complicated planning exercise. Should you go by boat, hovercraft, catamaran or even if you can wait a while, by Channel tunnel?

The advice of which method to choose depends on a number of things. For many, the crossing has to be as quick as possible — for reasons of time, or worries about spending that time afloat. If that is the case, the shortest routes are Dover to Calais or Boulogne in France; Dover to Ostende in Belgium; or Ramsgate to Dunkerque in France. By ferry, depending on the weather, these short crossings should take around an hour and a half.

Hovercraft are quicker but they can obviously take far fewer vehicles at a time, which may limit your booking, and they are more effected by the weather. A crossing by hovercraft is noisier and less relaxing than by boat, but it is certainly fast. Besides the hovercraft, Hoverspeed also now have the high tech and very impressive looking Sea Cat catamaran which travels from Dover to Calais and Dover to Boulogne. The Dover to Calais route can take as little as 35-40 minutes by Sea Cat or hovercraft.

The majority of travellers to Europe obviously use the ferries and for many this is an important — and enjoyable — part of the journey. If you are travelling to the popular Brittany area of France, or further south still to Spain and Portugal, then a ferry will transport you a considerable distance in comfort — often overnight. Cabins are not expensive and can make a significant difference to how you feel when arriving in mainland Europe. Such overnight crossings are also necessary when travelling to northern Europe and Scandinavia.

When it comes to planning your ferry crossing, it really is important to make your booking well in advance. Certain times of the year, especially during the school holidays, will see the most popular sailing times fully booked months in advance. If you are booking a crossing, you may need to be flexible.

As this book is being written, men are still busily scurrying away at the infamous Channel Tunnel, so it is difficult to offer any advice. Many travellers will flock to use this when it opens, just for the novelty value. However, many travellers may avoid the tunnel through claustrophobia or other worries. Whatever the case, the competition it should create with the ferry and hovercraft companies should benefit all European travellers.

Motorway signs throughout Europe can be interpreted using a little common-sense.

Right: **This Spanish motorway sign explains which vehicles are prohibited from using the motorway - and it does not include British tourists.**

Below,left: **This slip-road on to a motorway actually shows a Give Way sign for joining traffic.**

Below, right: **Always plan your route. This picture shows that the motorway is about to split. Which route do you need?**

Opposite: **Don't be confused by parking areas on motorways. These are not service areas and usually only have toilets and picnic tables. Great if you need a short break but not if you need fuel.**

Opposite: **As in the UK, motorway marker boards give you warning of approaching exit. This is a 300m board on a German autobahn.**
Second left: **Ausfahrt is German for exit. The graphic symbols are self-explanatory.**
Left: **When in Holland, the Dutch word for exit is Uit.**
Below left: **The end of motorway sign is normally the same as in the UK in most countries except that in Switzerland they have green motorway signs**

Don't let the surroundings confuse if you are looking for directions. A good driver always plans well ahead and keeps alert for the signs.

MOTORAIL SERVICES

You may also wish to consider beginning your European journey by motorail. This service is available at several of the ferry ports on the continent and from easily accessible major cities including Paris and Brussels. By travelling in this way you may arrive at your holiday destination more quickly and without being tired by a long drive. The expense of the fares can also be offset to some degree by savings in fuel costs and motorway tolls.

ADDITIONAL INSURANCE COVER

It may seem a little heavy-handed to stress the necessity for extra insurance cover, especially since we are telling you that driving in Europe is enjoyable and not a step into some dangerous unknown. The most significant point, however, is to consider the distance involved. A breakdown somewhere in Italy or up in the Austrian Alps can suddenly seem a long way from home. Minor breakdowns can always be repaired locally, but in the event of a major problem or accident, the need will be to get the vehicle home and that's when it starts to get expensive if you do not have any additional insurance cover.

If you are a member of either of the two main motoring organisations the AA or RAC, you will probably be familiar with their schemes. The AA's Five Star Service is a well-proven plan which offers a high level of cover for travellers throughout Europe. The scheme is structured for the motorist to take out cover for either the vehicle, the passengers, or both. You can have cover for exactly the number of days you are away. All policyholders are provided with a comprehensive assistance and information booklet packed full of detail and telephone numbers of AA offices throughout Europe. Contact the Automobile Association, Fanum House, Basingstoke, Hampshire, RG21 2EA. Tel: 0256 20123 or local offices.

The RAC offers similar overseas travel cover under the Eurocover Insurance scheme. Once again this can be tailored to suit which countries you intend to visit and how long you will be there. This is a very comprehensive and impressive service. Contact the RAC's travel service at RAC House, Bartlett Street, South Croydon, Surrey CR2 6XW. Tel: 081 686 0088 or local offices.

There is a lot to be said for being in a scheme from one of the top two companies, the costs involved will vary but are obviously very competitive. However, you could also consider contacting Europ Assistance (252 High Street, Croydon, Surrey CR0 1NF. Tel: 081 680 1234) who run a number of schemes. For an annual fee, Europ Assistance will cover you in the UK and allow you a number of days abroad in a year. National Breakdown have European extensions to some of their UK accident breakdown packages (National Breakdown, PO Box 300, Leeds, West Yorkshire, LS99 2LZ. Tel: 0532 393666). It obviously makes a lot of sense to shop around when looking for European cover, and you should make sure you explain exactly where you intend to travel; countries like Turkey, for example, may not be included in some of the schemes. Equally, if you are only going to France for two weeks, why pay for insurance cover that would bring your car back should it break down somewhere in the Swiss Alps? Choose wisely and then travel with peace of mind.

The Motorail Experience

By day or night, whether you are on holiday or on business, Motorail beats the motorway.
Simply take your car to the station where it will be put on the Motorail train – and leave the long distance
driving to us. On arrival you will be relaxed, refreshed and ready to go.

Motorail operates between London and Carlisle, Glasgow, Edinburgh, Fort William, Inverness
and Aberdeen – also between Bristol and Edinburgh.

Ring 0345 090700 (local call rate) for details and a copy of the Motorail brochure.

SALLY
FERRIES

The art of smooth sailing.

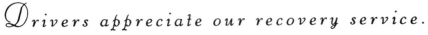

Drivers appreciate our recovery service.

When you've got a long way to travel, you need all the rest you can get. On Sally Ferries we go out of our way to help you make a full recovery. Pick up a Sally Ferries brochure from your nearest travel agent or call us direct on 0843 595522.

Driving on the Right

DRIVING ON THE RIGHT

For the reasonably experienced driver, much of what you do behind the wheel is instinctive. Good drivers will carry out the same actions when arriving at junctions, round-abouts and motorway slip roads every time. Even when you arrive at completely unfamiliar locations, your driving practices should not change. In short, once you have had reasonable experience driving on the left, nothing is really a problem.

But now you are going to be driving on the 'wrong side of the road'. The first most important point is not to worry about it. If you consider yourself confident 'on the left' then with a little advice and concentration, driving on the Continent of Europe will not cause any problems.

It is worth just mentioning a few basic words of advice before you roll off the ferry and take to the right for the first time. Are you sitting comfortably? On no account should you compromise your driving position to carry extra luggage or give someone extra leg room in the back.

The next point to note is mirrors. In this unfamiliar position on the road, your ability to observe everything that is going on around you is even more important. The most awkward manoeuvres are overtaking and turning left and so it is important that the mirror on your passenger's side is correctly adjusted. If your car does not have a mirror fitted there, you should seriously consider seeing if you can obtain a clip-on mirror before you leave the UK. Your main driving mirror will also have to be adjusted correctly. It may also be advisable to consider fitting one of the larger 'panorama' type mirrors to give you a better view.

When you disembark from the ferry, do not fall into the trap of meekly following the car in front. True, you could have a seasoned traveller ahead of you, an ideal 'instructor' — you could also have an idiot who has never driven on the right and has taken far less preparation than you. Make your own mind up on what you are going to do, don't just follow others.

Some drivers tend to 'hug' the kerb when they first venture on the right. This is natural since you may feel like keeping out of the way. Try and position yourself away from the kerb in the same position as you would at home — this obviously depends on the width of the road.

Your first important manoeuvre is likely to be **overtaking**, even if it is merely a parked car. This is where the mirror on your left is so useful, and you should also glance over your shoulder as well. Try not to let any of your passengers offer you advice — although this can be tricky if you have a dedicated 'back seat driver' on board. With the driver on the kerb side, overtaking in moving traffic can seem a little awkward at first, and the last thing you need is the person in the passenger seat shouting 'yes', 'no', 'clear, er sort off' as you attempt to overtake your first French truck. As the vehicle ahead will be blocking your view, it will be necessary for you to keep well back in order to see whether it is safe to pass.

Roundabouts are probably the next hurdle for the UK driver, since you have to go round them the other way! They really are no problem and follow much the same guidelines as the UK. The general rule is to give way to traffic on the roundabout as in the UK. Should it be otherwise,

Opposite, top left: **Road junctions need not confuse. Follow the markings.**
Opposite, lower left: **Of course, in heavy traffic, that's often easier said than done!**
Opposite, right: **Cobble-stone roads like these in Belgium, look quaint, but give a dreadful ride, and can be treacherous in the wet. Take extra care**
Left: **Remember that when you have pulled over, it is the front seat passenger that will alight 'into' the road. Be particularly careful if you have children in the back that they leave the car on the safe side.**

When driving in areas with cycle routes remember that you must give way to cyclists if you intend to cross the route.

traffic signs will inform the driver as you approach. It used to be in France that traffic entering the roundabout had priority but now, as you approach a roundabout you will often see the sign *Vous n'avez pas la priorité*, indicating that you do not have priority. Where the sign is not present, approach the roundabout with care since old habits die hard — harder still for ancient French farmers driving even more ancient Citroen 2CVs.

At major **junctions**, take some care when turning left. Quite often, especially in France, a left turn off a major route will involve you peeling off to the right, looping round and then stopping to cross the road as if you were sitting at a crossroads. This makes a lot of sense. You do not then hold up the traffic. Such junctions are clearly marked.

You should really be familiar with the vast majority of continental **road signs** since they are used throughout Europe. If you are at all unsure, grab a copy of the Highway Code and brush up on the signs like no stopping, no parking, no overtaking, right of way and motor vehicles prohibited. Many motorway service centres on the continent have

tourist offices and you can buy books that offer detailed advice and translations of road signs. However, anyone conversant with what you find regularly in the UK should have little difficulty reading the signs in mainland Europe. Even ones you may have never seen will be obvious since they are usually a graphic or drawing rather than words.

One of the most common mistakes for the novice European traveller happens when you return to your car. If you have stopped for some lunch or maybe just to admire the view, it is so easy for the concentration to drop, you jump back in the car and proceed to drive off down the wrong side of the road. Always remind yourself what side of the road you are driving on before you set off and indeed keep doing this as you travel along.

When **parking** always do so at a specified car park or service station if you can, and always make sure you park on the right hand side of the road. You are then far less likely to drive off on the wrong side. And when you leave your car unattended, never *ever*, leave your belongings in clear view. Take valuables with you, or stow them away locked in the boot. Your car is foreign now and will attract undesirables looking to obtain your holiday money, cameras and the like. It is so easy to forget this piece of advice and it could ruin your holiday.

Many European countries operate a 'Blue zone' parking system. These areas, often free of charge, are available for the touring motorist. You will be restricted in time to how long you can stay and will need to obtain an official parking disc to leave on display in your car. These parking discs can usually be obtained from tourist offices, post offices, some newsagents or by contacting the local police.

If you need to **hire a car** remember to have both your passport and recommended driving licence. The majority of countries dealt with in this publication will all have offices for the big hire companies like Hertz, Avis and Europcar, together with local companies. One advantage of the major 'named' companies is that they will often accept credit cards although the local hire car companies may well be cheaper. Always confirm that you have suitable insurance cover before accepting the deal. Remember also to say where you intend to take the car if you are considering crossing any national borders and make sure you have the necessary paperwork and cover.

We have listed all the national motoring organisations throughout Europe affiliated to either the FIA (Federation International de l'Automobile) or the AIT (Alliance Internationale de Tourisme). These organisations are recognised by both the AA and RAC.

MOTORWAY TRAVELLING

For many, European travelling involves a lot of time on motorways. The most common route is Calais down through France to the sunny Mediterranean on the *Autoroute del Sole*. In general terms, European motorway driving is very much like driving in the UK, although I have to say that in many European countries, lane discipline can actually be better than the UK - it is certainly better than much of what is experienced on the M25 or M1. You should certainly enjoy travelling on French *autoroutes*, Italian *autostrada*, and German *autobahnen*.

Most motorway signs throughout Europe are blue with white lettering, (Switzerland is an exception being green with white lettering). The rules regarding entering and leaving motorways are the same as in the UK, so bear in mind when you enter the slip road to join, that motorway traffic

This Italian signs tells drivers that the nearside lane is for taxis and buses.

Opposite: **Always fill up at regular intervals. That way you should be able to choose a known brand of fuel. Not everywhere accepts credit cards so always carry some cash (see individual country sections for more details).**
Left: **Even if you have not seen this sign before it's pretty obvious that it is telling you to keep away from the extreme edge of the road!**
Below left: **Most busy 'tourist traps' have suitable parking areas for you to stop in safety and have a look around but the British car and caravan moving off at the left of the picture will need to take care to join the correct side of the road.** *The Caravan Club.*

will be coming from your left and it has right of way. Stay in the inside lane for a short while to get used to the traffic and remember that you overtake on the left and that it is from the left that approaching traffic will overtake you.

Speed limits are different to the UK. Watch the signs carefully because if you are caught speeding in a number of European countries it is an instant on-the-spot fine. And the police will often insist on cash. Travellers cheques may be acceptable, or sometimes Euro Cheques, but your credit card may not do nicely. Most modern cars have kilometre per hour figures marked on the speedometer so you do not have to keep converting your speeds in your head. General advice on speed, however, is:

50kph (31mph) — in built up areas
90kph (56mph) — on single lane normal roads
110kph (68mph) — on dual carriageways
130kph (81mph) — on motorways

(We deal with more specific speed limits in each individual country's driving advice section.)

Distances throughout Europe are obviously given in kilometres so when you see your motorway exit coming up in 1km (or 1,000m), remember you do not have the same time to get ready to leave the motorway as you do in the UK when you see the 1mile junction signs. One kilometre is 5/8ths of a mile, so when you see the 1000m board, you want to be positioned in the correct lane ready for the exit.

Motorway **service areas** in Europe are very similar to those in the UK — although in many the food is better! Most are open 24 hours a day and offer a variety of services besides petrol, oil, toilets and a restaurant. Some have banking facilities, motels or tourist offices. In Western Europe payment can be by the major credit cards, travellers cheques and Euro cheques. As you move into Eastern Europe we would advise that you carry sufficient cash and travellers cheques for the journey.

The availability of leaded and unleaded **petrol** is good in Western Europe. There are generally three grades of unleaded fuel available often called Regular, Premium and Super. If the names differ, the best guide is price. Never use the lowest grade unless you have to. If your car uses leaded petrol, do not worry if you are forced to fill up with unleaded. If you really have to, however, always use the grade with the highest octane rating. No harm will be done but do make sure that the next fill-up is with the correct fuel. Similarly if by accident you fill-up with leaded in a vehicle that has a catalytic convertor, you will not destroy the catalyst. Fill-up with unleaded next time and all will be well — only repeated use of leaded fuel will harm the convertor.

Throughout Europe you will often see 'rest areas' marked off the motorway. These will be parking areas, often with toilet facilities, where you can stop for a break or have a picnic without having to leave the motorway.

When planning your journey, it may pay to follow the major International Routes. These are marked with a white letter E on a green background followed by a number. These routes cross international borders allowing you to follow the same road number across different countries. This is only really suitable in western Europe.

TAKING TOLL

If you are travelling in France, Spain, Italy, Greece and some Austrian routes, you will find motorway tolls are payable. Switzerland too, has a separate fee for driving on motorways (see page 92). A general rule to remember is that you will often need loose change to pay the motorway toll. When joining the motorway it will be necessary to take a ticket at the barrier. When you do so, remember that it records both your position on the motorway and the time you joined. When you then come to hand the ticket in at the motorway exit it is possible to calculate your average speed between the two points - and that can lead to a fine should it be proved you must have exceeded the limit! It is possible to use major credit cards at some toll booths, but we really do recommend cash as it is a lot quicker.

It is obviously difficult to give costs of motorway tolls throughout Europe due to fluctuations in exchange rates. For an up-to-date costing you can contact either the AA or RAC shortly before you leave. To give you some idea, however, as this is being written the cost of travelling from Calais to Cannes in the south of France in a car is 338 French Francs, approximately £35. In Switzerland, the annual motorway tax, known as vignette, is 30 Swiss

Francs which is approximately £15 - failure to display the tax sticker can lead to a fine of 100 Swiss Francs.

Besides tolls, Europe also has its fair share of **tunnels**. It is invariably an offence to drive through a tunnel without lights. There are often road signs to remind you, but failure to do so can lead to an on-the-spot fine. It is also an offence to stop or overtake. Always take off your sunglasses as you enter a tunnel so that your eyes can adjust quicker and keep a good 70m distance from the car in front - this is a safe distance and actually law in a number of European countries.

CROSSING INTERNATIONAL BORDERS

When you arrive at border crossings, make sure you are obeying the speed limits and slow down accordingly.

Europe is definitely 'opening up'. I have driven from England, through France and Belgium to arrive at my hotel in Germany having only shown my passport once - back at Dover. At many border crossings you will simply be waved through. If you are stopped, make sure that you have your passport(s) and vehicle's documents available for inspection and providing you are not carrying anything illegal, you will have no problems at all.

There have been significant changes in the duty-free allowances for motorists travelling within the EC. Provided the goods are tax-paid in the country of origin, and they are for your personal consumption and not for resale, you are free to have a great deal more than before. As this is being written, the EC has issued guidelines on what it considers non-commercial amounts. This includes some 800

Right: **When joining a motorway, you will often be asked to press the button to gain your toll ticket, this picture is from Italy. You keep this ticket and hand it in when you leave the motorway when the charge will be calculated.**
Second right: **If you are worried that you will not understand what the attendant says, fear not, since the toll will often be shown to you at the pay booth.**
Opposite: **As for toll bridges or tunnels in the UK, you will often be asked to pay a set rate, displayed as you approach the booth.**

cigarettes, 10 litres of spirits, 90 litres of wine and 110 litres of beer per adult. The traditional duty-free allowance for goods purchased on the ferry remains until July 1999. To avoid confusion, we advise you to study the customs leaflets as you leave the UK.

On your return, you will notice that the old 'red' and 'green' customs channels will have been removed which should speed up movement. However, don't forget that customs officials still have the right to stop you and search your car thoroughly.

Apart from the obvious cases of drugs, animals and firearms (!), it is worth noting here that there are a number of restrictions on the importation of meat, poultry and related products into the UK. It really is a simple matter of getting the correct forms on your way out of the UK so as not to have any problems on your return.

Some European countries have regulations regarding temporary introduction of car phones and citizens band radios. If possible, we would advise removal of these before you leave the UK.

And when you do return, we are also sure that you will want to go back to Europe. Having to drive on the right is no great problem. It does call for that extra concentration but you soon get used to it. And after driving around our crowded little island, Europe is a great place for the enthusiastic motorist and his family to explore.

Lézignan	22	34	44	13
Carcassonne est	34	53	68	20
Carcassonne ouest	34	53	68	20
Castelnaudary	47	73	94	28
Villefranche de L.	54	84	108	32
Toulouse sud-ouest	63	98	126	38
Toulouse sud-est	66	102	132	40

Autoroutes du Sud de la France

paiement en sortie

toll on exit

ticket

1500 m.

PEAJE TOLL

Opposite, left: **This is a French toll ticket machine. You will need to take a ticket actually to enter the motorway**

Opposite, right: **For longer distances, credit cards are often accepted. This is the approach to a French toll.**

Above left: **This overhead sign explains which lane you must go in to pay your toll and exit the motorway.**

Below left: **As fully explained in the text, if you are travelling through Switzerland you will need to purchase a *'vignette'* and display it in the corner of your windscreen.**

Towing & Caravans

TOWING ADVICE FOR CARAVANS AND BOATS

If you are considering taking your caravan into Europe, then it is likely that you will have experience of driving with one in the UK before you go. We do not have the space here to go into detail about towing a caravan, but do strongly advise all potential Continental caravanners to contact the Caravan Club before you leave for their advice. The Caravan Club, East Grinstead House, East Grinstead, West Sussex, RH19 1UA. Tel: 0342 326944.

All caravans, boats or trailers taken into Europe must have a unique **chassis identification plate.** These are available from the two motoring organisations before you leave. Don't forget that you will need a **GB** identification plate on both your car and your caravan or trailer.

You should fit additional mirrors to your car for towing in Europe. An additional mirror, or mirror extension, on your passenger's side is obligatory for towing a caravan in Italy and Denmark.

As you should in the UK, always remember other road users while towing in Europe. Leave a gap between yourself and other slow-moving traffic. *The Caravan Club.*

You should plan your route even more carefully if you are towing a caravan to avoid city centres. Caravans are actually banned from the centre of Paris - but you would need your head examined to try and take one there!

Take full advice from your insurance company if you plan to caravan abroad. In Austria, for instance, full insurance is needed for any caravan.

If you are wanting to tow a boat into Europe, some extra preparations are necessary. Your boat must be registered in the UK. This is possible through the Royal Yachting Association for a small fee. Remember to take the actual **registration certificate** with you as a photocopy is not acceptable. The only exceptions to the registration rule are very small craft that are to be used close to shore in France. A Topper dinghy does not need to be registered but a Laser does.

If you are taking your boat to Germany, Greece, Netherlands (with a speedboat), Spain, Portugal, and some parts of Italy, a Helmsman's Overseas **Certificate of Competence** is required Obviously it makes sense to contact the Royal Yachting Association before you leave. RYA, RYA House, Romsey Road, Eastleigh, Hampshire SO5 4YA. Tel: 0703 629962.

It is to be recommended to take Third Party **insurance** for the boat with you. This is compulsory for boats used on the Swiss lakes and compulsory in Italy for craft with engines above 3hp. Italy also requires a translation of the insurance certificate.

Some countries also require you to carry customs documentation for boats; again it is sensible to contact the RYA before embarking into Europe.

As in the UK there are different speed limits for drivers towing caravans. These instructions are clearly marked and should be adhered to thus avoiding the risk of those expensive on-the-spot fines.

CARAVAN TOWING

AUSTRIA
Cars towing a caravan under 750kg are restricted to 100kph (62mph) on all roads outside built up areas. In the Tyrol, the speed limit is 80kph (50mph) at all times.

Towing in the narrow winding streets of old towns should not be casually undertaken. Forethought when approaching a scene like this may pay off. *AA Photo Library.*

DENMARK
When towing, speed limits of 70kph (43mph) on motorways and main roads outside built up areas.

FRANCE
Speed limits are the same as for cars alone provided the caravan does not exceed the weight of the tow vehicle.

GERMANY
When towing, a maximum limit of 80kph (50mph) exists on motorways and main roads outside built up areas.

Remember those additional mirrors to aid driving and towing. *The Caravan Club.*

HUNGARY
When towing, speed limits are 80kph (50mph) on motorways, 70kph (43mph) on other main roads outside built up areas.

ITALY
Caravans are limited to 80kph (50mph) outside built up areas and 100kph (62mph) on motorways.

LUXEMBOURG
Cars towing are limited to 75kph (45mph) outside built up areas and 90kph (56mph) on motorways.

NETHERLANDS
Cars towing a single axle caravan are limited to 80kph (50mph) outside built up areas.

NORWAY
Cars towing caravans are limited to 80kph (50mph) outside built up areas.

PORTUGAL
Caravans are limited to 50kph (37mph) in built up areas, 70kph (43mph) on main roads and 90kph (56mph) on motorways.

SPAIN
Cars towing caravans are limited to 70kph (43mph) on main roads and 80kph (50mph) on motorways.

SWEDEN
A speed limit of 70kph (43mph) is fixed for cars towing caravans on all main roads including motorways.

SWITZERLAND
Cars towing a caravan up to 1,000kg are limited to 80kph (50mph) on all main roads outside built up areas including motorways.

TURKEY
Cars towing caravans are limited to 40kph (25mph) in built up areas and 70kph (43mph) on other roads.

In Case of Accident or Breakdown

Even people with the best prepared vehicles and most comprehensive preparations, can have problems. Accidents and breakdowns are facts of life, but when they happen in a foreign land, many miles from home, they can seem even worse.

In the event of your car breaking down, it is a case of using your commonsense and acting in much the same way as you would in the UK. Endeavour to get the car off the road if possible, use your hazard warning lights, and place your warning triangle in the appropriate position. On major roads this means 50m from the vehicle, on a motorway 150m. Take care to consider the position of your vehicle so that if necessary you put the warning triangle round a bend to warn approaching traffic.

If you are going to suffer a breakdown, it's going to seem a long way from home if you are without appropriate insurance cover.

Right: **This is NOT the way to use a warning triangle. Make sure you place it at least 50m from the vehicle so that approaching traffic has good warning.**
Second right: **This is the way to use a warning triangle; giving approaching traffic prior knowledge of the problem.**
Below left: **Should you breakdown just round a bend, put the warning triangle on the road in full view of approaching traffic.**
Below right & Opposite: **Look out for emergency telephones. If you use them, you will need details of your breakdown insurance. If you don't have any, you will need your wallet.** *AA Public Relations*

If the problem is one that you cannot solve, you will then have to consider what breakdown cover you took out back in the UK. If you are properly covered, it will be a case of making the necessary telephone call and waiting patiently for help to arrive. If you have no cover organised, you will need to find a local garage. If you cannot find one, try the local police who will obviously know the area. Most European motorways have emergency telephones as in the UK which will mean you will be able to be towed off the motorway, probably to a nearby garage or the next service area. If you thought breakdown insurance to be an unnecessary extra, it will be about now that you will be changing your view. We have made suggestions regarding breakdown insurance earlier in this publication.

ACCIDENTS DO HAPPEN

In the unfortunate occurrence of having an accident, it is once again much the same as in the UK. However, if you do not speak the local language, it can be extremely difficult. As anyone will tell you, the first words of advice are — *Don't Panic. Keep Calm.* Obviously, if people have been injured, then medical assistance is the first move. Emergency phone numbers are given in each country's entry in this book. In this section we will concentrate on the more frequent, minor accidents where the damage is purely to the vehicle.

It is always advisable to contact the police (compulsory in many countries) and report the accident. If you have to move your vehicle, either mark its position in the road before you do so or better still, take photographs from a variety of different angles

If a third party is involved you will need to exchange name and address and insurance details. It is here that you will be grateful for the Green Card that you obtained from your insurance broker in the UK. Make sure that you get all the necessary details from the other people and vehicles involved together with names and addresses of any independent witnesses. Write down the date time, place and weather conditions at the time. And don't forget the name and number of the policeman handling the incident. It's a good idea to make a little sketch of what happened as you saw it, marking both your speed and the speed of any other vehicles involved. Under no circumstances should you admit liability, or sign any statement without the advice of a lawyer or competent official.

When everything is sorted at the scene of the accident and you are on your way again, remember that you must contact your own insurance company. Do not wait until you get home.

When you think about it, taking out accident and break-down insurance is a must. Both the major motoring organisations offer comprehensive cover and you will get detailed information packs to take with you. These will also have the all-important telephone numbers relating to each European country for the emergency service and the local motoring organisations, the latter necessary to ensure you get those repairs done as quickly as possible so as not to interrupt your holiday too severely.

Far left: **Always make sure that you read the warning signs telling you when mountain passes are open for traffic.**
Left: **Some passes, like this at Grossglockner in Austria, will have a toll charge.**

Opposite: **At some passes there will be a barrier. If it is down you will not be allowed through. Then it's a case of turning round...**
Above left: **A toll charge will seem a small price to pay to get to some of Europe's most stunning scenery.**
Below left: **At some toll booths, maps and guides can also be purchased.**

1-Tages-Karte 340,-S
2-Tages-Karte 380,-S
Einzelkarte 260,-S

Key to Quick Reference Symbols:

 Minimum driving age 18

 Warning triangle compulsory

 First Aid kit compulsory

 Fire extinguisher compulsory

 Set of spare bulbs compulsory

 Green Card compulsory/strongly recommended

 International Driving Permit compulsory/strongly recommended

 Credit cards not widely accepted when buying fuel

 Illegal to care spare fuel can

 Dipped headlights compulsory at all times

Speed Limits Summary

A - B - C

A - Limit in built-up areas (kph)

B - major roads outside towns

C - motorways or equivalent

Some countries have additional categories of road and others apply variations at night or in poor weather. Speed limit signs are usually similar to those found in the UK and should, of course, invariably be obeyed.

Austria

    50 - 100 - 130

One of the major attractions for taking your car into Europe has to be the superb Alpine scenery that it can transport you to. And, of course, this is not limited to enthusiastic skiers. Driving round the Austrian Alps in the summer is a memorable experience, even if you don't see too much snow.

Most of the traffic regulations in Austria are similar to those in the UK. However, the minimum age for driving a temporarily imported car is 18 and it is strongly recommended that all drivers obtain an International Driving Permit as confusion over the British licence has been known. You should also carry your Vehicle Registration Document. **Children** under the age of 12 are not permitted to sit in the front (unless they are in special child seats) and the wearing of seat belts is obligatory. A **Warning triangle** and **First Aid Kit** are compulsory.

There are severe penalties for drivers who are found to have more that 0.08% alcohol in the bloodstream (0.04% in the breath). These include large fines and possible imprisonment, foreign drivers may be banned from driving in Austria if found to be over the limit.

Speed limits in Austria are generally similar to the rest of Europe: 100kph (62mph) on trunk roads; 130kph (81mph) on motorways; 50kph (31mph) for the built-up areas (between place name signs). These limits do change for cars with trailers and caravans. Austrian motorways are generally free of any charges but there are some tolls to be paid for certain mountain passes and road tunnels

Third Party **insurance** is compulsory and although a Green card is not, all major motoring associations strongly recom-

TRAVELLERS' TIPS

MOTORING ORGANISATIONS & ASSISTANCE
Österreichischer Automobil Motorrad und Touring Club, FIA & AIT, Schubertring 1-3, 101 Wien 1

ÖAMTC emergency breakdown service tel 120

EMERGENCY PHONE NUMBERS
Police 133
Fire service 122
Ambulance 144

FUEL AVAILABILITY
Regular unleaded (91 octane) Bleifrei
Eurosuper or Euro-95 unleaded
Supergrade leaded Verbleit
Diesel

Credit cards not acceptable at petrol stations

Parking free in 'blue zones'. Parking discs required

Minimum driving age 18

International Driving Permit strongly advisable

Warning triangle and First Aid Kit compulsory

mend that you carry one. Trailers must be covered by a separate policy. In the event of an **accident**, drivers must report to the police if there is injury to persons. The Austrian automobile clubs operate a 24 hour emergency breakdown service which is open to all.

Some care should be taken when **parking** in Austrian towns. 'Blue zones' with maximum free parking time of 90 minutes are clearly marked. Parking clocks can be obtained free of charge from tobacconists' shops (Tabak-Trafik). Some towns charge for parking and vouchers can be obtained from tobacconists, banks and petrol stations. These must be clearly displayed.

All **petrol stations** in Austria sell unleaded (bleifrei) and super unleaded petrol called EUROSUPER or EURO-95 together with supergrade leaded and diesel fuel and are clearly signposted. One important point, however, is that credit cards are not usually accepted for payment.

For many drivers, Austria means **Alpine driving** in the win-ter. Obviously you need some extra preparations for this. The Alpine roads are often narrow, but there is no firm rule for priority, it is a case of who can reverse into a passing point more easily. When the snows come, studded tyres are allowed (from 15th November to the 1st Sunday after Easter). Snow chains can be hired from the Austrian automobile club, OAMTC. Remember that if you know what the weather will be like before you leave, you can hire snow chains in the UK from the AA or RAC. Driving in these areas often means poor daytime visibility and dipped headlights must be used in these conditions. Parking lights only are used in built-up areas with all-night street lighting (a broad red band round a lamp-post means these street lights go out at midnight).

For the first time European driver, Austria may seem a long way to drive (the distance from Calais to Innsbruck is 700 miles). The scenery, however, is stunning and well worth all the time and effort, that's for sure.

Right & Opposite: **Breakdown services in action in Belgium and France.** *AA Commercial Services.*

Belgium

▲ 60 - 90 - 120

TRAVELLERS' TIPS

MOTORING
ORGANISATIONS &
ASSISTANCE
RACB Royal Automobile Club
de Belgique, FIA,
53 rue d'Arion,
1040 Brussels.

TCB Touring Club Royal de
Belgique, AIT,
44 rue de la Loi,
1040 Brussels.

Weather reports and road
conditions tel 991

EMERGENCY PHONE
NUMBERS
Police 101
Fire service 100
Ambulance 100

FUEL AVAILABILITY
Supergrade leaded (98-99
octane)
Regular unleaded (92 octane)
Unverbleit/Sans plomb
Super unleaded (95 octane)
Sans plomb Super
Diesel

Credit cards accepted at most
major petrol stations

Parking in 'Blue zones' in
some built-up areas with the
aid of parking discs

Minimum driving age 18

Warning triangle compulsory

Trams have priority

Belgium is one of the most under-rated countries in Europe for tourism. It has a lot to offer the traveller, with Brussels in particular being a wonderful city to visit. It is also not that far away, with ferry services from Dover direct to Ostend. The **minimum age** for a UK licence holder driving in Belgium is 18. Children under the age of 12 are not permitted to sit in the front seat if there is room for them elsewhere. Third Party insurance is compulsory and a Green Card recommended. On-the-spot fines are levied on offending motorists and an official receipt must be issued by the officer collecting the fine. The level of alcohol permitted in the bloodstream is 0.08%, penalties may include surrendering driving licence. A **warning triangle** is compulsory, First Aid Kit recommended.

The national speed limits are similar to the rest of Europe. As a general rule; 60kph (37mph) in built-up areas, 120kph (75mph) on motorways and dual carriageways, other roads 90kph (56mph). In normal circumstances there is a minimum motorway speed of 70kph (43mph).

There are some **priority** rules that need adhering to in Belgium. Some of the major cities have trams and they *always* have priority. At junctions and roundabouts with no signs to the contrary, you give way to the right. In built-up areas, buses leaving their stops have priority. You may also notice that people use their car horn when overtaking. This does not show a grudge against foreign tourists but is an accepted action when indicating your intention to overtake. It should only be done outside built-up areas.

In the major cities, 'Blue zone' parking areas exist. Parking discs can be obtained from police stations or offices of the RACB. Commonsense applies in many cases. Do not park in places where you would not park in the UK. Wheel clamps are used in Antwerp and Ghent.

In the event of an **accident**, if there are injuries, the police will insist the driver takes a blood alcohol test — failure to consent can lead to arrest. You must remain at the scene of an accident as long as required by the police.

Fuel available includes Super grade leaded (98-99 octane), Regular unleaded (92 octane) and Super unleaded (95 octane). Visa, Eurocard and Mastercard are accepted on motorway service areas and in the larger towns.

TRAVELLERS' TIPS

MOTORING
ORGANISATIONS &
ASSISTANCE
Union of Bulgarian Motorists
(SBA), FIA & AIT,
3 Place Positano,
1000 Sofia.

EMERGENCY PHONE
NUMBERS
Police 878011
Fire service 160
Ambulance 150

FUEL AVAILABILITY
Unleaded Bes Olovo or
Bleifrei
Super leaded (96 octane)
Super unleaded (93 octane)
Diesel

Petrol coupons available for
tourists

Use the blue petrol pumps

Need translation of UK driving
licence or International Driving
Permit

Warning triangle, First Aid kit
and fire extinguisher
compulsory

A road tax is payable by all
cars entering the country

Severe drinking and driving
restrictions

Bulgaria

| IDP | (18) | 🔥 | ▲ | 🧰 | GC |

60 - 80 - 120

There's no reason why you should not be that little extra bit adventurous and drive to Bulgaria. However, as it is a country that is not yet used to a massive influx of western tourists, you do need to ensure you have all the necessary paperwork. A UK **driving licence** is acceptable providing it has a **translation** certified by the Bulgarian Consulate or Embassy. If you do not have a translation, an International Driving Permit is necessary. It's not a bad idea to have both. The minimum driving age is 18. All cars entering the country have to pay a **road tax** (about £8 at the time of writing)**.**

Children under the age of 12 are not allowed to sit in the front seats. You must carry, a **fire extinguisher, warning triangle and First Aid kit** in the car. As a general rule, speed limits are lower than the rest of Europe — when you see some of the roads you will understand why. In built-up areas it is 60kph (37mph), outside built-up areas 80kph (50mph) and motorways 120kph (74mph). The police do impose on-the-spot fines. **Drinking and driving** are severely punished with the blood alcohol level only 0.03% permitted.

As well as the compulsory Third Party insurance, you must carry a **Green Card**. In the event of an accident where vehicles are seriously damaged , or persons injured, the police must be called.

In built-up areas it is prohibited to park in places that might obstruct traffic. There are no parking meters so always look for the international 'P' sign for safe parking.

Petrol coupons are used in Bulgaria. These are obtained at the border and throughout the country from banks and travel agencies. Take care always to buy the best quality petrol available — avoid Regular leaded as it is only 86 octane. Leaded Super (96 octane), and Unleaded Super (93 octane) are available. Tourists should look to use the blue pumps.

Obviously before leaving for Bulgaria you must contact the Embassy for up-to-date visa requirements. As this is being written, a tourist entry **visa** (valid for three months) is required by British Nationals. It is recommended that you obtain the visa before leaving the UK.

Cyprus

▲▲ ✖ 50 - 100 - N/A

There is obviously limited driving potential on the island of Cyprus due to its size, but what's available is impressive. You can drive from the sunshine of the Mediterranean beaches up into the snow-topped mountains in no time at all. Contact the national tourist office for ferry details. The other bonus is that Cypriots **drive on the left.**

A UK driving licence is accepted. Each car must carry **two warning triangles**. Speed limits are strictly enforced, it is certainly not the place for the driver in a hurry: built-up areas 50kph (31mph), outside built-up areas the limit varies between 60-100kph (37-62mph).

Any driving considered to be under the influence of alcohol will be subject to a blood test. Fines are imposed.

You will feel at home parking in Cyprus since they have **parking meters** in main towns. You must use your lights between half an hour after sunset and half an hour before sunrise.

It is prohibited to carry **spare fuel** in cans. Avoid Regular leaded fuel (87 octane), there is Super leaded (98 octane) and unleaded petrol is available in the larger towns.

Because of the very strong tourist industry many major credit cards are accepted.

TRAVELLERS' TIPS

MOTORING ORGANISATIONS & ASSISTANCE
Cyprus Automobile Association,
12 Chr. Mylonas Street,
Nicosia 141
tel 02-313233

FUEL AVAILABILITY
Regular leaded (87 octane)
Super leaded (98 octane)
Unleaded

Cypriots drive on the left

Two warning triangles compulsory

Prohibited to carry spare fuel in cans

Strict speed limits

Opposite: **Do not park or obstruct a cycle path**
Left: **An example, from the south of France, of the sort of parking that will not endear you to the locals.**

Opposite, top left: **A welcome reminder at the ferry port when starting your journey.**
Opposite, lower left & right: **There are many Blue Zone areas in Europe where you can legally park your vehicle.** *AA Public Relations.*
Left: **Never park where there is an obvious sign telling you not to do so!**

TRAVELLERS' TIPS

MOTORING
ORGANISATIONS &
ASSISTANCE
Ustredni Automotoklub CSFR,
FIA & AIT,
Cernomorska 9,
101 50 Prague 10.

For breakdown assistance tel:
773455

Information service for
tourists:
Autoturist,
Na Rybnicku 16,
120 76 Prague 2.
tel: 2-203 355

EMERGENCY PHONE
NUMBERS
Police 158
Fire brigade 150
Ambulance 155

FUEL AVAILABILITY
Leaded (90 octane)
Super leaded (96 octane)
Unleaded (96 octane) usually
marked 'Natural'
Diesel

Petrol coupons no longer
necessary

Unleaded and diesel stations
limited

Credit cards accepted in main
towns and tourist areas

Drinking and driving strictly
forbidden

Vehicle damage must be
reported to authorities

Warning triangle, First Aid kit
and replacement bulb kit
compulsory

Czech & Slovak Republics

IDP (18) GC ▲ ↻ 60 - 90 - 110

This is another eastern European country well worth visiting provided you make extra preparations before entering. At the time of writing it was not clear how the proposed separation of the Czech and Slovak republics would affect the visitor. Traffic laws are unlikely to change substantially, however. A UK driving licence should be accepted, but it is advisable to have an **International Driving Permit.** The minimum age for driving is 18. It is recommended to have a **Green Card** along with your compulsory Third Party insurance. Children under the age of 12 are not allowed in the front seats.

Besides the compulsory **warning triangle** and **First Aid kit**, you must also carry a set of **replacement bulbs**. On entering the country, any damage to your vehicle must be certified by the authorities at the border. If you damage your vehicle within the country make sure a police report is obtained because **damaged vehicles** cannot be taken out of the country without this evidence.

Speed limits are similar to other eastern European countries: built-up areas 60kph (37mph), outside built-up areas 90kph (56mph) and motorways 110kph (68mph). Some of these restrictions change during the night and early hours of the morning.

Drinking and driving is strictly forbidden, *any* evidence of alcohol in the blood can lead to prosecution. Police have the power to issue on-the-spot fines for motoring offenses. Parking is restricted throughout the country. It is only permitted on one side of the street (unless it is a one way street). Stopping and parking is prohibited in places where a vehicle might cause an obstruction.

Priority is generally the same as the rest of Europe, giving way to vehicles coming from the right. **Trams** have right of way and can only be overtaken on the right.

Petrol coupons are no longer necessary in Czechoslovakia. Try to avoid leaded Special (90 octane) and fill up with Super leaded (96 octane). Unleaded Super (96 octane) is available but restricted; you can get a map of suitable sta- tions at the border. Diesel is also limited throughout the country; look for signs TT Diesel. You can bring fuel in to the country duty free in a spare can (up to 20 litres) but it is prohibited to export fuel in a can

Visas are no longer required for British Nationals but it would pay to contact the Embassy for any changes before you leave — and to get a phrase book.

Left: **In many European countries it is important to park only on one side of the street as here in Prague.** *AA Photo Library.*
Opposite: **It may be more convenient and more fun when visiting Prague to leave your car and take a tram!** *AA Photo Library.*

Denmark

 50 - 80 - 100

If you are looking for real driving pleasure and excellent scenery, Denmark can be recommended. The standard of even the secondary roads is very high indeed.

As in the UK, the **minimum driving age** is 17 and a UK driving licence is sufficient. Third Party insurance is compulsory and a **Green Card** recommended.

The Danes are strict on the safety aspects of driving. **Dipped headlights** must be used 24 hours a day and you must adjust your headlight beam to suit. **Children** over three and under seven are not permitted to travel without suitable restraints. A **warning triangle** must be carried and a First Aid kit is recommended.

Below right & below: **Typical scenes on the excellent Danish roads.**

If you exceed the **speed limit** you can expect to be fined on the spot. Even minor offenses can lead to heavy fines. Built-up areas have 50kph (31mph) limits, outside built-up areas 80 kph (50mph) and motorways 100kph (62mph). Take care to follow the signs.

The level of alcohol in the blood permitted is 0.08%. There are severe penalties including licence suspension, fines and possible imprisonment.

Petrol stations sell many internationally recognised brands of fuel. Some are unattended with machines which use 50kroner and 100kroner notes. There are limited stations on the motorway network so fill up early. Major credit cards are often accepted at the larger stations. Recognised fuel grades available; Super leaded, Regular unleaded (92 octane) and Super unleaded (95 octane).

Rules regarding **priority** are similar to the rest of Europe; give way to traffic on the right, except on a roundabout where traffic already on roundabout has priority. Look out for a line of triangles (often referred to as shark's teeth) painted across a road indicating you must stop and give way. Give way to buses leaving their stops and only use your car's horn in case of danger.

Care must be taken with **parking**. As a rule it is permitted on the right side of the road. You should not stop or park close to junctions or exits from cycle paths or if the kerb near a bus stop is yellow. Unlawful parking will lead to your car being towed away. Parking discs are required in areas where limited parking is available and these can be obtained from petrol stations, post offices and tourist offices. There are also parking meters in major towns.

TRAVELLERS' TIPS

MOTORING
ORGANISATIONS &
ASSISTANCE
Forenede Danske Motorejere,
Firskovvej 32,
PO Box 500,
DK-2800 Lyngby.
tel: 45 93 08 00

Breakdown advice:
Dansk Forening for
International
Motorkoretojsforsikring,
Amaliegade 10,
DK-1256, Copenhagen
tel: 33 13 75 55

EMERGENCY PHONE
NUMBERS
Police 112
Fire service 112
Ambulance 112

FUEL AVAILABILITY
Super leaded (98 octane)
Regular unleaded (92 octane)
blyfri benzin
Super unleaded (95 octane)
Diesel

Some major credit cards
accepted at petrol stations.
Some stations unattended
and accept notes

Speed limits strictly enforced

On-the-spot fines enforced

Warning triangle required

Dipped headlights to be used
at all times

Left: **Entering Denmark you are given a great deal of information from this one sign explaining speed limits in different areas, plus the compulsory use of seat belts and dipped headlights**

Opposite, left: **A graphic method of showing you that you must slow down when you enter this Danish town.**
Opposite, right: **Show consideration for pedestrians, even if you can't think of them, as partners.**
Top left: **You do not need to speak the language to understand that this sign is trying to ensure you travel sensibly and do not race.**
Below left: **Watch out, young children about.**
Top right: **This sign is imploring people to give better signals so that everyone understands what is happening.**

MOTORING
ORGANISATIONS &
ASSISTANCE
ATCF Autoliitto, FIA & AIT,
Kansakoulukatu 10,
00101 Helsinki
tel (90) 6940022.

Finnish Motor Insurers'
Bureau
(Liikennevakuutusyhdistys),
Bulevardi 28,
00120 Helsinki.

EMERGENCY PHONE
NUMBERS
see instructions beside public
telephones
or, Helsinki only:
 Police 000
 Fire service 000
 Ambulance 000

FUEL AVAILABILITY
Regular leaded (92 octane)
Normal

Super leaded (99 octane)
Unleaded Lyijyton
Diesel

Major credit cards often
accepted

Dipped headlights to be used
24 hours a day outside built-
up areas

Severe penalties for drinking
and driving

Snow tyres necessary in
winter

Report all accidents involving
elk or reindeer

Finland

(18) ▲ 🄌 ◗≣ 50 - 80 - 120

If the idea of driving around a beautifully lakeland land-scape appeals, Finland is a must. Add to this the fact that the northern part of the country crosses the Arctic Circle and you have a marvellous land for the European motorist. Obviously, because of its location, some extra preparations are necessary before you go.

A UK driving licence is accepted in Finland with the mini-mum driving age 18. Third Party insurance is compulsory and a **Green Card** recommended. A **warning triangle** and **First Aid Kit** are both recommended. **Dipped headlights** must be used at all times outside built-up areas. There are no regulations regarding children travelling in the front seats, although seat belts must be used at all times.

There are severe penalties for drinking and driving with only 0.05% alcohol present leading to a heavy fine, 0.15% lead-ing to possible imprisonment.

Finland follows most of Europe with priority from the right being the general rule unless indicated to the contrary by a yellow triangle sign. In Helsinki, trams always have priority, as do buses leaving their stops in areas with 60kmh speed limits. Throughout the country the general speed limits are 50kmh (31 mph) in built-up areas, between 80-100kmh (50-62mph) outside built-up areas and 120kmh (74mph) on motorways.

The rules for **parking** follow commonsense. There are park-ing meters in main towns. On-the-spot parking fines are levied and these have to be paid at post offices, banks or by post.

All the major grades of fuel are available at most **petrol stations**. Regular leaded (92 octane) and Super leaded (99 octane) are available as well as unleaded. Many petrol sta-tions close at 21.00 each night. Visa, Eurocard and Master-card are accepted in payment.

If you are involved in an **accident** it is essential that you notify the Finnish Motor Insurers' Bureau, the Liikennevaku-utusyhdistys, which deals with accidents involving foreign vehicles. One rather unique hazard is wildlife. In the south elk, and in the north reindeer, can often be seen wandering across the road. These are large animals and a collision is usually serious. All accidents with elk or reindeer must be reported to the police.

In December, January and February it is highly recom-mended that you fit **snow tyres** to your car (and caravan). Studded tyres can be hired within Finland, but our advice is to contact one of the major motoring organisations before you leave the UK. With proper preparations a driving holi-day through Finland can be very rewarding.

France

   18   ▲   ◝   50 - 90 - 130

For many, taking your car abroad simply means driving in France. And what a superb touring country it is. If France is your first taste of European motoring, you will not be disappointed. There is an excellent motorway (*autoroute*) system crossing the country — albeit a toll motorway — plus some gloriously quiet country lanes. One word of advice, however; the French enjoy motoring too, so it pays not to travel through France during the national holiday periods (particularly the beginning and end of August and 14 July).

Your full UK licence is accepted but the minimum age for driving is 18. A **Green Card** is not compulsory but to be recommended since Third Party insurance in France offers less cover than the UK. Equally a **warning triangle** is not compulsory if a car has hazard warning lights, but it is to be recommended since electrical problems can make these lights inoperative. It is also sensible to carry a **replacement bulb set**. Again it is not compulsory, but it is illegal to drive a car in France with faulty lights. **Children** under 10 may not travel in the front unless in a specially approved seat. Your vehicle will be allowed in to France if fitted with a car telephone but its use is prohibited.

The drink driving is the same level as the UK at 0.08%. On-the-spot fines are payable and can be very severe, especially for speeding. **Speed limits** are clearly marked throughout. The general limits are 50kph (31mph) in built-up areas, 90kph (56mph) outside built-up areas, 110kph (68mph) on dual carriageways and 130kph (81mph) on motorways. In **wet weather** these limits outside built-up areas are reduced to 80kph (49mph), 100kph (62mph) and 110kph (68mph) respectively. Visitors who have held a driving licence for less than one year must not exceed 90kph (56mph) or any lower speed limit. On the Paris *Périphérique* urban ring road there is an 80kph (50mph) speed limit — although on occasion you will wonder if the French actually know that!

The French motorway speed limit is 130kph in good conditions, but it drops to 110kph in the rain.

Right: **As in the UK, you must give way when joining a French roundabout.**
Opposite, all four: **French autoroute signs indicating that you must keep your distance. The chevrons painted in the road allow you to judge carefully the interval between you and the car in front.**

On many single track roads you will see a solid white line down the middle. This indicates that you should not over-take and cross the line. Failure to observe this can lead to the driver being heavily penalised.

Travelling throughout France is likely to include motorway driving. The country has a **toll** road system, so make sure you budget for this in your route planning. You can pay for these tolls on most major credit cards. Many short sections of toll motorways are automatic and take small change, so keep some in the car.

All major grades of fuel are widely available throughout the country. Diesel is sold as gas-oil or gaz-oil. Most major credit cards are accepted at the majority of stations.

You will need to adjust your car's **headlight beams**. You will find beam convertor sets are available at ferry ports before your departure and are easily fitted to your car's headlamp lenses. There is no longer a legal need to have yellow headlight beams. One important point to note, how-ever, is that if a French driver flashes his lights, he is *not* asking you to go first. He actually expects you to let *him* go first.

There are **parking** areas designated and it is usually obvi-ous where not to park. Do not park where the kerbs are marked in yellow. Some roads in central Paris are now no parking areas and while in the capital, do not leave your car in the same place for more than 24 consecutive hours. In

58

TRAVELLERS' TIPS

MOTORING
ORGANISATIONS &
ASSISTANCE
Automobile Club de France,
FIA,
6-8 Place de la Concorde,
75008 Paris
tel: 42 65 34 70.

ACN Automobile Club
National, FIA & AIT,
9 rue Anatole de la Forge,
75017 Paris
tel 42 27 82 00.

EMERGENCY PHONE
NUMBERS
Police 17
Fire service 18
Ambulance if no number
given, call police

FUEL AVAILABILITY
Leaded Essence Plomb
Unleaded Sans Plomb
Diesel Gas-oil

Major credit cards accepted

Minimum driver age 18

Warning triangle and
replacement bulb set
recommended

Speed limits drop in wet
weather conditions

Headlamp beams must be
adjusted (Yellow tinted
headlights no longer
compulsory)

Motorway toll roads

Heavy on-the-spot speeding
fines

many larger cities the European 'blue zone' parking scheme operates, which means parking discs are needed. These can be obtained from police stations and tourist offices.

Driving in France has few fears for the competent UK driver. The infamous *priorité à droite* on all roads no longer occurs - this was where cars from the right *always* had priority, even when they were coming from a minor road. Now traffic on major roads has priority and the vast majority of junctions and crossroads are well-signposted. In the event of no signs, you give way to traffic coming from the right. Approaching roundabouts, you will regularly see the sign, *Vous n'avez pas la priorité* explaining that traffic joining the roundabout no longer has priority and that you wait for a suitable gap as you do in the UK. It pays to take a little care in some of the rural areas — where old habits die hard — but really, there's no problem.

Traffic lights have a subtle difference in that the amber light does not go on between red and green. When the amber light flashes you can proceed with caution. Also, at junctions you may well have a flashing yellow arrow which is indicating that you can turn in the direction of the arrow while giving way to traffic and pedestrians where necessary.

If you have never been to Europe with your car, it's a good idea to make France your first move.

Second left: **Red lights mean stop whatever the country. Watch out for the regularly used Continental practice of overhead traffic lights.**
Left: **This French road junction shows a flashing amber turn signal. This means that you can turn if no traffic is approaching.**
Below left: **Flashing amber lights highlight this pedestrian crossing.**

Opposite, left: **An excellent illustration of why it may be best to avoid driving in central Paris, the Champs Elysee seen from the Arc de Triomphe.** *AA Photo Library.*
Opposite, right: **Priority is clearly indicated at this typical major junction in France.**

TRAVELLERS' TIPS

MOTORING
ORGANISATIONS &
ASSISTANCE
ADAC Allgemeiner Deutscher
Automobil-Club, FIA & AIT,
Am Westpark 8,
8000 Munich 70
tel (089) 76760.

AVD Automobil-Club von
Deutschland, FIA & AIT,
Lyonerstrasse 16,
6000 Frankfurt am Main 71.
tel: (069) 6606-0.

EMERGENCY PHONE
NUMBERS
Police 110
Fire service 112
Ambulance 110

FUEL AVAILABILITY
Leaded Verbleit
Unleaded Bleifrei
Diesel

Major credit cards accepted
(in east Germany, travellers
cheques more acceptable)

Be aware of speed limit signs

Warning triangle compulsory

First Aid kit and set
replacement bulbs
recommended

Carry an insurance Green
Card

Fast moving traffic on some
motorway roads

On-the-spot fines imposed

Germany

50 - 80 - 130

With the two former German states now united as one, there's a lot more for the European motorist to explore. This makes the Federal Republic of Germany an exciting new opportunity.

A UK licence is acceptable and it is recommended that you carry an insurance **Green Card**. Children under 12 cannot travel in the front seats unless special child seats are fitted. A **warning triangle** is compulsory and visitors are strongly advised to carry a First Aid kit and set of replacement bulbs.

As this is being written there is a slight discrepancy regarding the permitted level of alcohol in the bloodstream. In West Germany it must not exceed 0.08%, but in the former GDR the level is zero. As always, the answer is not to drink and drive.

Germany has an excellent motorway (autobahn) system of some 10,500km, with 169 service areas and 268 service stations. The motorways are toll free and are open 24 hours (except in exceptional circumstances). All major grades of fuel are available and the majority of major credit cards are acceptable.

Do not be misled by the sometimes held view that German motorways do not have **speed limits**. There are some sections that do not have an upper limit but these are becoming increasingly rare. However, do keep an eye in your rear-view mirror on the motorway as fast approaching cars in the left hand overtaking lane can catch you out. Motorway discipline in Germany is good, but some vehicles do travel quickly at times. The standard motorway limit for private cars without a trailer is 130kph (80mph). On non-motorway

roads outside built-up areas the limit is 80kph (50mph) and in built-up areas 50kph (31mph).

However, as this book was being written, there were a few discrepancies regarding speed limits. The motorway limit in the old GDR was 100 kph (62mph) and for other main roads outside built-up areas 80kph (50mph). The advice has to be to be vigilant with speed limit signs at all times, especially when in the eastern side of the country.

The major German motoring association, the ADAC, has **emergency patrols** on motorway and major roads. In the event of a breakdown, assistance can be summoned by

Far left: **Always try to be in the correct lane and be guided by the road markings as here in the former East Berlin.**
This page, both: **Flashing road signs can be used to indicate a particular hazard, like a sharp bend or significant speed limit.**

telephone (small arrows marked on posts indicate the nearest phone). Make sure you ask for *Strassenwachthilfe* (road service assistance). The ADAC also runs an emergency service to relay radio messages to motorists and messages can be handed in at any ADAC office or police station.

The police can impose on-the-spot fines for exceeding the speed limit, parking offenses, having under-age children sitting in the front seats, using abusive language and running out of fuel on the motorway.

Priority regulations match the general rules of Europe, so give way to traffic coming from the right. In cities, trams do not necessarily have priority, but buses do when leaving bus stops. You must give way to a bus if the driver has signalled that he is leaving the kerb.

As the new Federal Republic of Germany is effectively the joining of two countries that in the past have been very different, you will undoubtedly still notice a big difference between west and east. Some of the main roads in west Germany, particularly in the tourist areas, are of very high quality. In the former GDR, unleaded petrol may be less commonly available, so carry a spare can, and payment here could be a lot easier with cash.

TRAVELLERS' TIPS

MOTORING
ORGANISATIONS &
ASSISTANCE
A M Capurro and Sons Ltd,
(RAC agent)
20 Line Wall Road,
Gibraltar.
tel 74813

FUEL AVAILABILITY
Unleaded
Leaded
Diesel
Petrol stations do not accept
credit cards

Highly advisable to park and
walk or take organised tours

Main road from Spanish
border crosses airport runway,
so watch out for traffic lights

Gibraltar

At six square kilometres, Gibraltar is hardly the ideal place for a touring holiday. Far better to arrive, park and walk or get local tours. However, it is certainly an interesting place to visit if you are in southern Spain.

A UK licence is accepted, a Green Card recommended and the minimum age for driving is 18.

Petrol stations do not accept credit cards, and there are only eight anyway. Due to the limited space, speed limits are low 30kph (20mph), and you are encouraged to **park** and investigate on foot or by organised transport. You can drive to the top of the Rock but the roads are very narrow and it is advisable to take an official tour. Most of the central shopping area is pedestrianised.

Both right: **Speed limits are often indicated by flashing road signs as are major crossroad junctions.**

Greece

      50 - 80 - 100

TRAVELLERS' TIPS

MOTORING
ORGANISATIONS &
ASSISTANCE
ELPA The Automobile and
Touring Club of Greece, FIA &
AIT,
2-4 Messogion Street,
115 27 Athens.
tel 779 1615

In the event of a breakdown,
ELPA runs a 24-hour service
that covers both the mainland
and the islands of Crete and
Corfu.
tel 104

Hellenic Touring Club, AIT,
12 Politechniou Street,
104 33 Athens
tel 52 40 854

EMERGENCY PHONE
NUMBERS
Emergency numbers vary
from place to place - see local
information. For Athens and
some other major locations
numbers are: Police 100; Fire
199; Ambulance 166

FUEL AVAILABILITY
Regular leaded (84 octane)
Super leaded (92-95 octane)
Unleaded Amoliwdi wensina
Diesel

Credit cards can be used at
some major stations

Minimum driving age 17

Warning triangle, First Aid kit
and fire extinguisher
compulsory

Do not use undipped
headlights in towns

Illegal to carry fuel in spare
can

Travelling to Greece poses no particular problems, even if it is quite a way from the English Channel. Ferries from Italy are available but the land route via Yugoslavia is no longer practical. A UK driving licence is accepted, although an International Driving Permit is to be recommended, and the minimum driving age is 17. You need to carry a **warning triangle, fire extinguisher** and **First Aid kit**. A Green Card is also to be highly recommended. Children under 10 are not permitted to travel in the front seats.

When crossing the border please note that it is illegal to carry fuel in spare cans. All major grades of fuel are available and universally known as Regular (84 octane) and Super (92-95 octane, leaded), Unleaded and Diesel. Avoid the Regular leaded if possible because of its low octane level. Some **petrol stations** in major cities will accept credit cards

When in towns and cities, it is illegal to use undipped headlights. When **parking** on a public road it is necessary to have a red rear light. Parking in Greece follows the international conventions. In Athens things get a little more hectic. There are parking meters and some special parking areas for visitors. If you park illegally, police may remove your registration plate.

Speed limits generally follow the rules of 50kph (31mph) in built-up areas, 80kph (50mph) outside built-up areas and only 100kph (62mph) on motorways. Greek police will impose fines for traffic offenses but they do not collect the fines themselves. Drinking and driving limits are lower than the UK at 0.05% of alcohol in the bloodstream.

There are some **toll** roads in Greece along the major motorway stretches and you will need to pay in Greek Drachmas.

Hungary

Another of the eastern European countries that will check the condition of your vehicle on entry. If you have suffered any body damage, make sure you obtain a police report on entering the country.

It is compulsory to have an **International Driving Permit** with your UK licence. The minimum age for driving is 18.

Third Party insurance is compulsory and we would strongly recommend a Green Card. You will not be allowed to enter, or leave, Hungary carrying spare fuel in a can but it is permitted to carry petrol in a can while in the country.

On motorways and in the larger towns, a lot of **petrol stations** are open 24 hours. Availibility of fuel types is indi-

Right: **The busy and exciting road and tram junction outside Budapest's Western Railway Station.** *AA Photo Library.*
Opposite, left: **Parking on only one side of the street in Budapest. Watch out on those cobbles if it rains.** *AA Photo Library.*
Opposite, right: **The busy Chain Bridge across the Danube linking Buda and Pest.** *AA Photo Library.*

MOTORING ORGANISATIONS & ASSISTANCE
MAK Magyar Autóklub, FIA & AIT,
Rómer Flóris utca 4/a,
Budapest II
Tel 1152 040

MAK breakdown service
tel 1/691 831

EMERGENCY TELEPHONE NUMBERS
Police 007
Fire service 005
Ambulance 004

FUEL AVAILABILITY
Regular leaded
Unleaded Olommentes uzemanyag
Diesel

AFOR and SHELL stations
Accept Eurocard

International Driving Permit required

Warning triangle compulsory

Strict drink driving laws

Report all accidents to police

cated by a white sign with a blue border showing two petrol pumps — black means leaded, green means unleaded. Petrol stations showing the AFOR and SHELL signs accept Eurocard.

In the event of an accident, make sure you report any damage to the police and the Hungarian State Insurance Company within 24 hours. You need a statement from the police otherwise you could suffer lengthy delays at the border.

Drinking and driving has very severe penalties, the blood alcohol limit is nil.

Do not use full **headlights** in built-up areas. If your car is fitted with additional Stop lights you are advised to disconnect them since they must not be used. Use of a car's horn is limited, not being permitted in built-up areas at night and banned completely in Budapest.

Right: **Speed limits and European radar in action. Keep to the limit.**

Second right: **Keep to the limit and do not use your car's horn - even if the locals still do; this is Italy after all.**

Below right: **Throughout Europe you will regularly see the 90kph limit sign on two-way, single carriageway roads.**

Opposite, top: **Quality motorways will often allow you to travel at 130kph.**

Opposite, bottom: **The majority of Europe uses blue signs on their motorways. However, if they are green signs, you're in Switzerland.**

TRAVELLERS' TIPS

MOTORING
ORGANISATIONS &
ASSISTANCE
ACI Automobile Club d'Italia,
FIA & AIT,
Via Marsala 8,
00185 Rome
tel 06 49981

TCI Touring Club Italiano, AIT,
Corso Italia 10,
20122 Milan
tel 02 85261.

For breakdown advice contact
tel 852663

EMERGENCY PHONE
NUMBERS
Police 113
Fire service 113
Ambulance 113

FUEL AVAILABILITY
Leaded Con Piombo
Unleaded Senza Piombo
Diesel

Credit cards are not accepted
at petrol stations

Some non-motorway service
stations closed on Sundays

Illegal to carry fuel in a spare
can

Check whether your licence
needs a translation or carry an
IDP

Pre-paid Viacard available for
motorway tolls

Lock away your valuables out
of sight

Italy

⑱ GC ▲ ✖

50 - 90 - 130

Taking your car to Italy is a particularly fulfilling experience, especially if you route your journey across the Alps. The country has a great deal to offer the motorist, that's for sure.

It is important that you have the correct driving licence. If you still hold one of the older, all green, UK driving licences, it is necessary for you to get an Italian translation (available from the major motoring organisations). The pink EC type UK licence does not need this translation. Once again, therefore, an International Driving Permit, although not compulsory, will ensure you have no problems. The minimum driving age in Italy is 18. A Green Card is recommended, and note that Third Party insurance is also necessary for boats used in Italian waters (see page 31).

A **warning triangle** is compulsory, and a set of replacement bulbs to be recommended. Children between the ages of 4 and 12 can be carried in the front or rear but must have a suitable child's restraint.

The Italian road system offers great variety. The motorway (autostrada) network is a toll system. You can pay with cash or purchase a Viacard which is rather like a season ticket. These are available from motorway toll booths or from tourist offices, post offices and some banks. The Viacard does mean you don't need extra cash in the car while travelling on the autostrada.

You will find all major grades of fuel available throughout Italy. **Petrol stations** are open 24 hours on motorways but on other roads they often close in early evening. Also, around a quarter of stations throughout Italy close on Sundays. Credit cards are not accepted for payment. As it is illegal to carry fuel in a spare can, it pays to take a little care and watch your fuel gauge!

Italians have something of a reputation when it comes to driving. In major cities it can be something of an experience, but if you have driven all the way to Italy, you will be quite experienced yourself. **Priority** is much the same as the rest of Europe, generally giving way to traffic from the right. On mountain roads, if you see a sign that looks like a horn or bugle in a red circle, it means that the post bus has right of way and you must stop, if necessary, to let it pass. You must always use your **headlights** in tunnels, even if they look well lit. Don't use your horn in built-up areas.

Speed limits throughout Italy match what is the general rule throughout Europe; 50 kph (31mph) in built-up areas, 90kph (56mph) outside built-up areas. On motorways the speed limit is split: 110kph (68mph) for cars up to 1,100cc, and 130kph (81mph) for cars over 1,100cc. Fines are made on-the-spot and can be particularly heavy for speeding and drinking and driving. The maximum allowed alcohol limit in the bloodstream is 0.08%

Italy has a number of the European 'Blue zones' for **parking**, which means you need to obtain a parking disc (available from petrol stations and the Italian motoring organisations). There are also 'Green zones' in major cities where parking is strictly prohibited between 0800-0930 and 1430-1600 on weekdays. The most important point regarding parking in Italy, however, is that you should NEVER leave any valuables visible in your car. Car crime is very prevalent in Italy, so if you cannot take it with you, lock it away out of sight.

Luxembourg

Blink and you will drive through Luxembourg, well not quite. Although small, it is a very picturesque part of Europe.
Minimum age for driving on a UK licence is 18. A **warning triangle** is compulsory and a First Aid kit recommended. Children under the age of 10 are not allowed in the front seats. There are severe drinking and driving penalties and the limit of alcohol in the blood is 0.08%. A Green Card is also recommended. All grades of fuel are available. Most petrol stations will accept Visa and Eurocard. You can also pay with Belgian francs. It is illegal to carry fuel in a spare can in the car.

'Blue zone' **parking** is used, together with parking meters in Luxembourg City. Illegally parked vehicles will be clamped and some cars are impounded. Side lights are required when parking if there is no public lighting. Many drivers flash headlights when overtaking at night outside built-up areas.

TRAVELLERS' TIPS

MOTORING ORGANISATIONS & ASSISTANCE
ACL Automobile Club du Grand Duché de Luxembourg, FIA & AIT,
13 route de Longwy, Helfenterbruck, Bertrange.
tel 450045.

EMERGENCY PHONE NUMBERS
Police 012
Fire service 012
Ambulance 012

FUEL AVAILABILITY
Leaded
Unleaded sans plomb
Super unleaded
Diesel

Visa and Eurocard accepted for payment

Illegal to carry fuel in spare can

The sign *Let Op* beside this junction in Luxembourg means that drivers turning must give way to pedestrians.

Travelling across Europe you will undoubtedly cross a great many railway lines. The European method of highlighting level crossings does vary a little from country to country and place to place with different combinations of red lights, bariers and other signs. However, they are all simple to understand even for the novice, as this selection from France, Italy and Switzerland shows.

At different border crossings you will see the necessary road requirements for the country. Always take note when crossing borders.

Netherlands

 (18) ▲ 50 - 80 - 120

TRAVELLERS' TIPS

MOTORING
ORGANISATIONS &
ASSISTANCE
KNAC Koninklijke
Nederlandsche Automobiel
Club, FIA,
Westvlietweg 118,
Leidschendam.
tel 070 399 7451.

ANWB Koninklijke
Nederlandsche
Toeristenbond, AIT,
Wassenaarsweg 220,
The Hague.
tel 070 314 7147

Breakdown assistance can be
obtained by calling ANWB

EMERGENCY PHONE
NUMBERS
see local directories

FUEL AVAILABILITY
Leaded Super
Unleaded Loodvrij
Diesel

Most stations accept the
major credit cards

Minimum age for driving 18

Caution for cyclists and
special road requirements for
large number of cyclists

Dipped headlights compulsory
in bad weather

Calling itself the 'Flower of Europe' the Dutch landscape may be flat but it is far from boring. If you are an horticultural enthusiast, it can be blooming colourful at times.

It is also one of the European countries that you can reach by ferry direct from the UK, so it will be many drivers' first taste of continental motoring. A UK driving licence is accepted but an International Driving Permit is advisable. The minimum age for driving is 18. Children under the age of 12 are not permitted to travel in the front, with the exception of children under 4 sitting in a special baby seat. You must carry a **warning triangle** and a First Aid kit is advisable. The alcohol in the blood limit is lower than the UK at 0.05% and severe penalties occur for drinking and driving offenses.

You will have no problems finding all grades of fuel and the vast majority of **petrol stations** accept credit cards. As this may be the start of your very first European journey, take care to observe the **speed limits**. They follow the general rule that is reflected throughout the continent. In built-up areas, 50kph (31mph), outside built-up areas 80kph (50mph), although the Dutch motorway limit is a little lower than France and Germany, at 120kph (74mph). There is a minimum speed on motorways of 70kph (44mph).

If you see diamond-shaped road signs, orange in colour with a white border, that explains you are on a major road and have **priority**. If you join a major road, give way to traffic from the right. The Netherlands is famous for its cyclists — and you will see a lot — take care when approaching some junctions if there is an obvious cycle-way running parallel with your road. In certain junctions, cyclists travel-

ling straight ahead have priority over all other traffic. Buses have right of way leaving bus stops in built-up areas.

Look out for a blue sign with an emblem of a white house. You will see this in built-up areas and it indicates caution; it can mean children playing in the street, pedestrians have right of way, or bicycles from the right have priority.

Parking follows the rules you will be familiar with. The Dutch also have the 'Blue zone' parking scheme operating and you will need to get a parking disc, available from police stations. There are also parking meters in major towns and cities.

There are some **toll** bridges in the Netherlands. However, these are relatively inexpensive.

These triangular road markings used in the Netherlands indicate that you must give way at the junction.

Right: **Map books at the ready.** The French motorway routes are signposted in blue and the other main roads in green, minor roads in white. The yellow sign with the black bar means that the road you are on no longer has priority. This sign is found in most European countries.

Below, both: **All Give Way signs are triangular** whether they are Switzerland or Spain as in these pictures.

Opposite: **This is another sign** throughout Europe. It means that you are on the priority road, therefore traffic joining should have to give way.

Right: **As the road bends round, the sign indicates that it remains the priority road.**
Below right: **Make your mind up; the road now splits and you can either go straight ahead or turn right. This is Vienna.**

Norway

  50 - 80 - 90

A journey to the Scandinavian countries can be very enjoyable indeed. If you are considering Norway, contact the Norwegian Tourist Board to get details of ferries or advised routes from the UK.

Once there, a UK licence is accepted. The minimum age to drive is 17, but you have to be 18 before you can hire a car in Norway. While not compulsory, it is recommended that you carry a warning triangle, a set of replacement bulbs and a First Aid kit. You must carry an insurance **Green Card**

Drinking and driving regulations are very strict, the limit of alcohol allowed in the blood is 0.05%, heavy fines can be expected and possible imprisonment. Police can impose fines on the spot for traffic violations.

Make sure you drive with **dipped headlights** at all times, even in bright sunlight. Parking is strictly controlled. Do not park on main roads or where there is a sign *All stans forbudt* (No stopping allowed). In major towns there are parking meters. Many of these are very sensibly colour-coded to indicate to drivers the period of time covered; yellow —

1 hour, grey — 2 hours and brown — 3 hours.

Speed limits on motorways and major roads are lower than many areas of Europe at 90kph (56mph). For built-up areas it is 50kph (31mph) and outside built-up areas 80kph (49mph). There are a large number of tunnels in Norway and some of these are **toll** tunnels. Some tolls are payable for drivers wishing to enter major cities like Bergen, Oslo and Trondheim.

You will find all the necessary grades of fuel. **Petrol stations**, however, are often closed during the evening and overnight and at weekends (open in densely populated areas). The major credit cards are accepted at the larger stations.

Obviously because of Norway's location, the weather can bring difficulties and it is against traffic regulations to attempt to travel without suitable tyres. **Winter and studded tyres** will be necessary during certain times of the year. Contact the major motoring organisations for full details of what is required explaining exactly when you intend to travel.

MOTORING ORGANISATIONS & ASSISTANCE
KNA Kongelig Norsk Automobilklub, FIA, Drammenasveien 20-C, Oslo 2.
tel 02 56 1000

NAF Norges Automobil-Forbund, AIT, Storgt. 2, Oslo 1.
tel 42 9400

In case of a breakdown contact:
Falken Redningskorps A/s Oslo
tel 02 23 2585

EMERGENCY PHONE NUMBERS
Police 002 (Oslo)
Ambulance 003 (Oslo)
For Fire service and numbers outside Oslo see local information

FUEL AVAILABILITY
Leaded (98 octane) Super
Unleaded (95 & 98 octane)
Blyfri
Diesel

Major credit cards accepted at larger stations

A lot of petrol stations closed at weekends

Green Card compulsory

Dipped headlights to be used at all times

Winter tyres necessary at certain times of the year

TRAVELLERS' TIPS

MOTORING
ORGANISATIONS &
ASSISTANCE
PZM Polski Zwiazek
Motorowy, FIA & AIT,
66 Kazimierzowska Street,
PL-02-518 Warsaw.

In case of a breakdown
contact PZM
tel 981

EMERGENCY PHONE
NUMBERS
Police 997
Fire service 998
Ambulance 999

FUEL AVAILABILITY
Leaded Etylina (86 and 98
octane)
Unleaded Benzyna bezolowiu
(available at certain stations
only)
Diesel ·

Major brands at stations on
main motorway routes

Green Card compulsory

Dipped headlights compulsory
between Nov — March

Poland

    *winter months

This eastern European country is well worth a visit and is not as far away as many people might think. The minimum age for driving is 18. A UK licence is acceptable but it is advisable also to carry an International Driving Permit. It is compulsory to have an insurance **Green Card** when entering the country. Children under the age of 10 are not permitted to travel in the front seats. A **warning triangle** is compulsory and a set of replacement bulbs recommended. Drinking and driving has severe penalties. Only 0.02% alcohol in the blood is permitted.

Second left & Opposite: **As in the UK, European motorway systems also have roadworks at times! Slow down and follow speed limit signs.**
Left: **Europe has its fair share of trams**

Traffic rules and regulations match most of continental Europe and you will be well experienced by the time you reach the Polish border. The majority of petrol stations in Poland are state-owned, but there is an increasing number of privately-owned stations setting up offering familiar grades of petrol. It is possible to buy leaded petrol of only 86 octane which is not recommended, so stick to the brands you recognise if possible. Unleaded petrol is not available everywhere, again stick to the major stations along the motorway and main road system. A lot of stations close in the evening and are only open for a few hours on Sunday. However, it is permitted to carry fuel in a spare can.

The major Polish motoring organisation has a reasonable breakdown service operating around major towns. If you have an accident you must report it to the police.

Speed limits match those of the rest of Europe. However, the minimum speed on a Polish motorway is 40kph (yes, that's only 24mph)!

Between November and March it is compulsory to use dipped headlights at all times.

Opposite: **The red overhead sign warns drivers that the left-hand lane is closed.**
Left: **Roadworks ahead, funnel into one lane and slow to the new speed limit.**
Below left: **Watch the overheads so you know when to move over into the green lane.**

TRAVELLERS' TIPS

NATIONAL MOTORING
ORGANISATION: ACP
Autómovel Club de Portugal,
FIA & AIT, Rua Rosa Araujo
24-26, 1200 Lisbon.
tel: 563931

EMERGENCY PHONE
NUMBERS
Police, Fire brigade and
Ambulance tel: 115

PETROL STATIONS
Leaded Gasolina
Unleaded Sem Chumbo
Diesel Gasoleo

Some credit cards accepted
for petrol but a surcharge is
levied

Speed limit for drivers who
have held licence for less than
a year

Full inventory for caravan
contents

Portugal

 ▲

A motoring holiday along the Algarve is obviously to be recommended, even if Portugal doesn't have the best roads in
Europe!
A UK licence is accepted and the minimum age is 17. However, some local difficulties have been known since the
Portuguese minimum is 18. An International Driving Permit
is recommended. If the vehicle is not registered in your
name, you will need a special certificate, an *Autorizacao*,
before you enter the country. Contact one of the major
motoring organisations.
A **warning triangle** is compulsory and an insurance Green
Card strongly advised. Children under 12 are not permitted
to travel in the front seats without suitable child seat
restraints.
Petrol stations have all major grades of fuel and some are
open 24 hours. Credit cards are often accepted , especially
Visa, but there is a surcharge on their use. When parking
make sure your car faces the same direction as the traffic.
Portugal has 'Blue zone' parking and discs are available
free from the ACP or police.
If you have held a full licence for less than a year, you are
restricted to a 90kph (56mph) maximum speed and your
car must carry a yellow disc showing '90'. Discs are available at ACP border offices. Some toll charges are levied on
stretches of the *autoestradas*.
If you are entering Portugal with a **caravan**, a full inventory
of the contents must be provided (forms are available at the
border).

Right: **Children painted in the
road like this obviously
means slow down since you
are approaching a school**

Romania

TRAVELLERS' TIPS

MOTORING
ORGANISATIONS &
ASSISTANCE
ACR Automobil Clubul
Roman, FIA & AIT,
Str. Tache Ionescu 27,
70154 Bucharest 22.
tel 15 55 10

In the event of a breakdown
contact the ACR tel: 12345

EMERGENCY PHONE
NUMBERS
All services 061 (Bucharest)
 06 (other towns)

FUEL AVAILABILITY
Leaded
Unleaded Benzina fara plumb
Diesel

Get a map of all PECO
unleaded petrol stations at the
border

Green Card insurance
compulsory

Strict drink driving laws

Traffic entering a roundabout
has priority

This is one European country much in the news over the last few years. And for sure, the country is keen to encourage tourists with a lot of unspoilt countryside on offer.

It is advisable to have an International Driving Permit and the minimum age to drive is 18. It is compulsory to carry the insurance **Green Card. A warning triangle and First Aid kit** are compulsory. Children under the age of 12 are not permitted to travel in the front seats.

It is said to be illegal to drive a dirty car! What is certain, however, is that if you have any damage to your vehicle, you should make sure that it is certified by the authorities as you enter. If you have an accident in Romania make sure you inform the police and get a certified report.

Unleaded fuel is available but it is limited. You can get a map of the necessary PECO petrol stations that have unleaded at the border. Carrying fuel in a spare can is permitted, and is therefore advisable.

Drinking and driving is strictly forbidden, there being no legally permissible amount of alcohol in your blood.

Most rules regarding **priority** are as the rest of Europe but please note that on roundabouts the traffic entering the roundabout has priority. So watch out for cars entering from your right. **Speed limits** are generally lower than the rest of Europe. Always park in the direction of traffic.

Far left: **Traffic queues ahead: time for a break perhaps?**
Left: **Two lanes into one ahead so be ready to allow traffic to merge.**

A series of warning signs.
Right: **Depending, of course, on the time of year and the weather, this road can be slippery and prone to ice.**
Below left: **And this one can cause you some distress! Verglas is probably best translated as 'black ice', a potential risk in any language.**
Below right: **Approaching a school so take care.**
Opposite: **Caution Low Flying Aircraft**: stop if the red lights flash and let the plane land.

Opposite: **Although you would never know by this sunny photograph, this sign tells you to beware high winds, heavy rain, snow and slippery road conditions.** *AA Public Relations.*

Second left: **You are on the main road and there are some main roadworks up ahead.** *AA Public Relations.*

Left: **This Czech sign warns drivers that the steep gradient may well cause problems for drivers with heavy loads.**

Below left: **It makes it a lot easier when they print the signs in English too!**

Planning should start with a call to the Foreign and Commonwealth Office Travel Advice Unit 071 270 4129; the Russian Embassy, London, 071 229 8027; and then contact a specialist travel agency like Intourist, London, 071 538 5965.

Russia (CIS)

 IDP ▲ 🏠 ⊡

Right: **Now this is what driving in Europe is all about, a pass through northern Spain's Cantabrian Mountains.** *AA Photo Library.*

Not for the faint-hearted, perhaps, but certainly not impossible. Obviously a journey to what many will still call Russia does involve some advance planning. You will need a Visa, and to obtain one you have to show an itinerary of exactly where you intend to go and book your accommodation in advance. Motorists actually require a special *Autotourist* visa, and you will be restricted to 300 miles a day.

A UK driving licence is not accepted, an **International Driving Permit** is compulsory. British insurance is not recognised, neither is the European Green Card, so you will need to organise extra insurance before your trip. A **warning triangle**, **fire extinguisher** and **First Aid kit** are required by law. However, you are advised to take a comprehensive kit of spares and accessories.

Fuel can be a problem since there is a shortage. Your vehicle will need to run on petrol with an octane level as low as 76 octane. Petrol coupons are issued at the border and you are recommended to carry a number of spare fuel cans.

Travellers cheques are not widely accepted and credit cards are only used for scraping off the ice. US dollars in small denominations are necessary.

Spain

 IDP (18) GC

50 - 90 -120

MOTORING ORGANISATIONS & ASSISTANCE
RACE Real Automóvil Club de España, FIA & AIT,
José Abascal 10,
Madrid 3.
tel 447 3200

EMERGENCY PHONE NUMBERS
see local directories OR
Madrid and Barcelona only,
  Police 091
  Fire service 2323232
  Ambulance 092

FUEL AVAILABILITY
Leaded Normal, Super Gasolina
Unleaded Sin Plombo
Diesel

Limited use of credit cards

Green Card and Bail Bond strongly recommended

International Driving Permit or translation of UK driving licence recommended

Set of replacement bulbs compulsory

As a country that has been very popular with UK tourists for many years, you may well be considering a driving holiday in Spain. Southern Spain is quite a long drive if you take the route from northern France, so it's well worth booking an overnight ferry crossing that takes you further south.

A pink EC type UK licence is officially all that is necessary. However, it is strongly advisable either to take an **International Driving Permit** or obtain a Spanish translation of your licence. The minimum age for driving is 18. Children under 12 can only travel in front seats if fitted with approved child restraints.

You should not travel to Spain without a **Green Card** insurance and a **Bail Bond**. Neither is legally compulsory but without them you may have serious problems should you be involved in an accident. Both are available from your insurers. A warning triangle is recommended, a **replacement set of bulbs** is compulsory.

Unleaded fuel is readily available at petrol stations in the tourist areas, and on the *autopista* motorway network, but less widespread elsewhere. Similarly, the use of credit cards for payment is more likely to be acceptable in the tourist areas.

Speed limits and priority follow the general rules throughout the rest of Europe; in built-up areas 50kph (31mph), outside built-up areas 90kph (56mph) and 120kph (74mph) on motorways. The majority of Spanish motorways are of the toll variety. You should give way to traffic from the right. When overtaking outside built-up areas, it is customary either to use the horn or flash your lights. Also, when over-taking outside built-up areas, it is permissible to increase your speed to 20kph over the statutory speed limit.

Parking is allowed in the standard European 'Blue zones'. The parking discs are available from hotels and travel agencies. On-the-spot fines can be made for traffic offenses and they must be paid on-the-spot unless you can name a person or company in Spain who will guarantee payment. You should always obtain an official receipt.

Left: **And even the more congested bits can have their attractions. This is the famous Roman aqueduct at Segovia.** *AA Photo Library.*

TRAVELLERS' TIPS

MOTORING
ORGANISATIONS &
ASSISTANCE
Motormännens Riksforbund,
AIT,
Sturegatan 32,
Stockholm.

KAK Kungl Automobil
Klubben, FIA,
Gyllenstiernsgatan 4,
S-11526, Stockholm

For breakdown advice contact
freephone: (020) 910 040

EMERGENCY PHONE
NUMBERS
Police, fire and ambulance
90000

FUEL AVAILABILITY
Leaded Bensin
Unleaded Blyfri 95
Diesel

Credit cards accepted at
many stations

Self-service petrol stations
accept Krona notes

Use dipped headlights at all
time

Climbing lanes aid overtaking
slower vehicles

Caution for wildlife needed on
some roads

Sweden

 ▲ 50 - 70 - 110

'Beware of Moose' is not something you are warned every day, but Sweden has much to offer the motorist.

A UK driving licence is accepted and the insurance **Green Card** recommended. Visiting motorists do not have to carry a warning triangle but it is advisable. Children of 7 or younger are not permitted to travel in the front seats unless in a special child seat. You must use **dipped headlights** at all times, even in bright sunlight.

All major grades of fuel are readily available but away from 'larger' towns, **petrol stations** are often not open 24 hours. Credit cards are accepted and there are many self-service stations that take Krona notes (although these rarely dispense Diesel).

Due to the topography, many Swedish roads have an extra lane provided for climbing steep hills. These are for faster traffic to use to overtake slower vehicles and should not be confused with UK crawler lanes. Similarly, Swedish roads often have wide shoulders. You will find that slower traffic will move on to these shoulders to allow you to pass. If you are towing a caravan, it is your responsibility to move over to make it easier for faster traffic to pass. In general, **speed limits** are 50kph (31mph) in built-up areas, 70kph (43mph) on busy roads outside built-up areas, otherwise 90kph (56mph). On motorways the limit sometimes rises to 110kph (68mph). The police can impose on-the-spot fines but they do not collect them.

As with all Scandinavian countries, there are very strict drinking and driving rules with only 0.02% alcohol in the blood permitted.

It is possible to get maps showing **parking** availability in

Stockholm and other major cities from local motoring organisations. In cities parking meters are often provided. You should be cautious when driving in the countryside because wildlife often crosses the roads and accidents with moose and deer can be very dangerous. Due to the severe climate in winter it is advisable to contact one of the major motoring organisations regarding the need for winter/snow tyres and snow chains.

Opposite: **Not a particularly inviting sight. Make sure you use dipped headlights.**
This page: **These tunnels have rules and regulations that must be complied with.**

TRAVELLERS' TIPS

MOTORING
ORGANISATIONS &
ASSISTANCE
ACS Automobile Club de
Suisse, FIA,
39 Wasserwerkgasse,
3000 Berne 13.
tel (031) 22 47 22

TCS Touring Club Suisse, AIT,
Rue Pierre-Fatio,
1211 Geneva 3.
tel (022) 37 12 12

General touring information
tel 111
Weather reports tel 162
Mountain pass conditions tel
163

EMERGENCY PHONE
NUMBERS
Police 117
Fire service 118
Ambulance 144

FUEL AVAILABILITY
Leaded Essence Plomb
  (Lausanne area)
Verbleit (Zurich area)
Con Piombo (Locarno area)
Unleaded Sans Plomb
  (Lausanne area)
Bleifrei (Zurich area)
Senza Piombo (Locarno area)
Diesel

Petrol stations accept credit
cards

Some automatic self-service
stations take Swiss franc
notes

Must carry a motorway tax
sticker

Snow chains needed during
winter season

Switzerland

   50 - 80 - 120

A country of fabulous mountain scenery, well worth a visit whatever the time of year.

A UK driving licence is acceptable and the minimum age for driving is 18. A **warning triangle** and a **First Aid kit** are both compulsory and it is recommended that you carry an insurance Green Card. Children under the age of 12 are not permitted in the front seat unless using a suitable child's restraint.

The most important point to driving in Switzerland is the need to pay the necessary motorway tax to gain your **'vignette'** sticker which must be displayed at all times when you use the motorway system. You will need a second vignette if you are towing a boat or caravan. These stickers can be purchased at the border, or can be obtained from the Swiss Tourist Office before departure. Drivers are fined for non-display.

Speed limits are those generally accepted throughout Europe; 50kph (31mph) in built-up areas, 80kph (50mph) outside built-up areas but only 120kph (74mph) on motorways.

Major grades of fuel are widely available. **Petrol stations** are not always open 24 hours, but some self-service stations accepting Swiss franc notes remain open. Some motorway self-service stations even have automatic pumps that accept credit cards.

Always use **dipped headlights** when entering tunnels — you can be fined for failing to do so. Many Swiss mountain roads are very narrow so caution is needed. When two cars meet and there is no obvious place to pass, the descending car must keep to the extreme right and stop if neces-

sary. Postal coaches have priority on these roads at all times. A sign showing a wheel wrapped in chains obviously means that **snow chains** will be needed for the road ahead. It is advisable to have hired these chains in the UK; contact one of the major motoring organisations.

Switzerland runs the European 'Blue zone' parking system and parking discs can be obtained from both motoring organisations, the ACS and TCS, and some petrol stations.

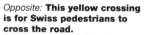

Opposite: **This yellow crossing is for Swiss pedestrians to cross the road.**
Top, left: **In places like Zurich, drivers have trams to contend with as well as pedestrians.**
Top, right: **A bus and cyclists ahead so take care.**
Below: **Wonderful scenery but watch out for others enjoying it too.**

For the UK driver, having to contend with trams for the first time can be a little bewildering. Just remember that they are not going to swerve out of the way! In most countries they have priority in the majority of road situations.
Tram signals are regular features throughout Europe. Trams are not all bad news. They offer a great method of transport. Find that parking space and take a tram ride. You won't regret it
AA Photo Library, p 95 below

TRAVELLERS' TIPS

MOTORING
ORGANISATIONS &
ASSISTANCE
TTOK Turing Ve Otomobil
Kurumu, FIA & AIT,
Halaskargazi Cad. 364.
80222 Sisli,
Istanbul.
tel 1314631

EMERGENCY PHONE
NUMBERS
contact local information

FUEL AVAILABILITY
Leaded
Unleaded Kursunsuz benzin
Diesel

Credit cards not accepted for
fuel

Fill up regularly, few petrol
stations off main roads

Report all accidents to the
police

Turkey

IDP   (18)   ▲   🗲

It is approximately 3000km from London to Istanbul, which means you will need some time to drive to Turkey. However, the Turkish people are extremely friendly and a holiday there has much to recommended it. The country is wonderfully mountainous and it will take you some time to travel from one place to another. You will need a Visa to enter the country, but at the time of writing this is merely a case of handing over £5 at the border.

A UK licence is accepted, but an International Driving Permit is advisable. The minimum driving age is 18. It is compulsory to carry a **warning triangle**, **fire extinguisher** and **First Aid kit**. It is also strongly recommended that you carry an insurance Green Card. If you are involved in an accident, you *must* inform the police as a report has to be completed.

Petrol stations are not that widespread so you are advised to top up regularly and keep to the main roads. Unleaded fuel is available but prices are often variable. You can carry fuel in a spare can.

Turkey uses the European international road signs and priority goes to vehicles coming from the right. Take care to note that *Park Yapilmaz* actually means No Parking.

Yugoslavia

Travel into or through what was known as Yugoslavia was not possible as this book was being compiled. Motorists are advised to call the Foreign Office Travellers Advisory Service on 071 270 4129 for further information.